ZEN AND
THE ART OF POTTERY

Zen and the Art of Pottery

by Kenneth R. Beittel

New York · WEATHERHILL · *Tokyo*

First edition, 1989

Published by John Weatherhill, Inc., of New York and Tokyo, with editorial offices at 8–3 Nibancho, Chiyoda-ku, Tokyo 102, Japan. Protected by copyright under terms of the International Copyright Union; all rights reserved. Printed in Korea and first published in Japan.

Library of Congress Cataloging in Publication Data: Beittel, Kenneth R. / Zen and the art of pottery / by Kenneth Beittel.—1st ed. / p.   cm. / Bibliography: p.   / 1. Arita porcelain—Religious aspects—Buddhism. / 2. Potters—Psychology. / 3. Zen Buddhism—Psychology. / I. Title. / NK4399. A7B45   1988 738′.01—dc19 / 88–105 CIP / ISBN 0–8348–0221–X

Contents

Preface

When I became an apprentice to the Arita tradition of porcelain pottery, I experienced what it means to be on such a path. Potters everywhere have been touched by this spiritual feeling; they would understand, therefore, the significance of the Buddha's silent gesture of holding a flower before his disciples as his total sermon. Here, in the act that might be said to be the origin of Zen, is the silent witness that potters instinctively grasp. Listen to Kabir, in his poem "The Clay Jug."

Inside this clay jug are canyons and pine mountains,
And the maker of canyons and pine mountains!
All seven oceans are inside, and hundreds of millions of stars.
The acid that tests gold is there and the one who judges jewels.
And the music from the strings that no one touches, and the source
    of all water.
If you want the truth, I will tell you the truth;
Friend, listen: The God whom I love is inside.[1]

In touch with the elements—earth, water, air, and fire—the potter in a very earthy and physical sense earns his honest touch of mysticism. His knowledge is not abstract but peculiar to art, and realized in action. In our time, however, when the traditions of handwork are endangered by anonymous products of little intrinsic worth; when mass media bombard us, turning us into passive spectators; when computerization speeds up the diminution of the human touch; when we can no longer hear the voices of individuals—in such a time even the potter runs the risk of forgetting what the ancient rites and trials symbolized.

Although it was in Japan that, twenty-one years ago, I learned first-hand the connection between Zen and the art of pottery, even there traditions are under threat. The irony of Japan's success in the technological sphere is that is it has led to the attrition of local tradition and spiritual initiation. The situation in America, while no better, is not bleak. Many Americans are restless and desirous of self-discovery and self-actualization, as thousands of self-help, pop psychology, and Eastern lore books demonstrate. Serious thinkers see signs of change all around. George Vithoulkas, a well-known medical doctor in Athens, recently wrote: "I strongly believe that humanity is entering a New Age in consciousness, a new understanding of things, making deep changes, re-evaluating accepted norms—in short, that there has been a deep and sincere revolution leading to a spiritual evolution unprecedented in strength and eagerness until this time."[2] Ken Wilber, in his 1981 book *Up from Eden,* made the same claim: the average level of consciousness has evolved to the highest point in humanity's history.[3] The new age heralded by such writers points toward more unification of the body-mind, and thus toward more creative imagination.

Introduction

After a time of decay comes the turning point.
The powerful light that has been banished returns.
There is movement, but it is not brought about by force. ...
The movement is natural, arising spontaneously.
For this reason the transformation of the old becomes easy.
The old is discarded and the new is introduced.
Both measures accord with time; therefore no harm results.[1]

I Ching

This is a book about Zen and the art of pottery. The practice of art as seen here is a spiritual discipline that offers a powerful antidote to an age suffering from its loss of center. It is also a harbinger of the way of art for a new age. In this coming age we will see a big shift in human consciousness, away from the mental, egoistic, toward more spiritual ways of being and knowing. Where Zen and art coexist, the call of the spirit is heard again in the land. To practice thus is to work at self-transformation: a transformation of one's entire being—not by increments, but by a quantum leap. This is an art for a new age.

Zen is the most ideal spiritual path for this reorientation. Its influence is pervasive in Japan in the practice of traditional arts. What I call the "great tradition" in pottery is rooted in both Eastern and Western traditions. It is an implicit community of workers of hand and wheel, of all those who have felt the stirrings of this art in a way honoring the holistic participation of body-mind in clay. It is a community of initiates on a path of self-formation, of consciousness expansion.

In this book I talk about initiation into the mysteries of this path, first through reference to Zen as encountered in a Japanese pottery tradition; and second, through an expansion of that view into the widest planetary perspective. In Zen Buddhism there is a striking expression, *honshō myōshū*, which roughly means "wondrous practice is original enlightenment." This means that with the right mind, right attitude, and right practice, the potter creates through his work the discipline that is already the expression of enlightenment. Thus the creation of pottery as spiritual practice is not a means to the attainment of enlightenment, it already is enlightenment.

It is not easy to let spontaneity arise from discipline, to stand within the world's great tradition. The late Hans Coper, a contemporary British potter, said that working on the wheel in the twentieth century made him feel "like a demented piano tuner striving for a phantom pitch."[2] But, he continued, "in working, one deals with facts." How true. These facts—of matter, muscle, body, form, and fire—are the very things that "break the bottom out of the bucket," as the Zen saying goes, so that practice indeed becomes original enlightenment.

I know that the attitude endorsed here can be mind-boggling. My pots are as good as I can make them, but since that is never good enough, I sometimes try to make them less so—like a part of nature, an object, a twig, a rock—each of which simply is, without any self-conscious thought of beauty. The hope is that such pieces were created in a complete simplicity, in an innocence of intention, under a paralysis of trying too much, too hard. Then, in truth, I would be living the meditator's cogito: I am not, therefore I am that. I have become one with nature, and in so doing, "the visible order of the universe is but the reflection of an invisible order" (Hermes Trismegistus). In this way the literal, figurative, and transcendent become one; speaking, signifying, and concealing become one; nature, the human, and the divine become one—for the pottery initiate on a spiritual path has learned to "speak" on all three levels at once. The uninitiated can hear one of these levels—perhaps two—but never all three.

Wallace Stevens, in "Anecdote of the Jar," intuitively demonstrates the tie between pottery and nature:

> I placed a jar in Tennessee,
> And round it was, upon a hill.
> It made the slovenly wilderness
> Surround that hill.

The wilderness rose up to it,
And sprawled around, no longer wild.
The jar was round upon the ground
And tall and of a port in air.

It took dominion everywhere.
The jar was gray and bare.
It did not give of bird or bush,
Like nothing else in Tennessee.[3]

This reflects a very Zen mood: with its pervasive influence, the jar brings together the sprawling wilderness. The wildness is tamed, and though unchanged, it is now part of an ecstatic and unified qualitative experience.

In part 1 of this book, I examine the broad scope of pottery and the great tradition. In chapter 1, I reflect on clay as a symbol of elemental wholeness. Through poetic description and reverie, I set forth a wide-ranging view of pottery and tradition. I then concentrate on roundness and centering, connecting these with the experience of wholeness missing from our modern lives. In chapter 2, I look at tradition through the world of Japanese ceramics. I describe the Arita tradition of porcelain and the master potter Manji Inoue. This tradition is also related to the practice of Zen.

Chapter 3, "The Community of Work," is an exploration of the meaning of true community and of the importance of experiencing community in modern life. Here I describe common labor and work as the humble but essential foundation for this exceedingly physical art. The Zen attitude is that sweeping out the studio or chopping wood are tasks as essential as any other within the practice of pottery. Special communal projects, such as kiln building and wood-firing, are also described.

Part 2 is devoted to practical discipleship, and the five chapters there encompass much more than technique. The rather precise descriptions are meant to convey to the general reader as well as to the beginning or advanced potter the direct interplay between practice, tradition, and the disciplined attitude that creates spontaneity from inside action. In the novice or someone outside tradition, such knowledge may exist only as a kind of intuition or expectancy; its possession primes the imagination and brings the keenest possible attention to feeling and sensation. It is in this sense that Aristotle said that accidents—that is, spontaneous and happy ones—fall toward the trained hand. So I have given clear, direct descriptions of these processes; they are the injunctions that point to the intimate knowledge experienced in practice. Just as there are ritual and instruction in *zazen* (Zen meditation) or yoga, so too are they present in an ancient, yet living, pottery tradition. Whereas it is most natural to learn through observation and imitation, I have worked here at a translation of acts into words.

In rites of initiation there are levels of practice and testing. And levels of practice are never finished or left completely behind, for whether in beginning or advanced lessons, the simplest of acts can manifest the sum total of the mysteries of the art, its tradition, indeed the consciousness to which they lead. Beginning forms of pottery remain a challenge toward perfection for initiate and master alike. What began as simple continues as simple, but the complexity it reveals is boundless. I have had beginning potters realize this in a flash of insight.

It is true, nevertheless, that advanced lessons assume relative mastery of beginning ones, and so, just like stages of initiation, the lessons are hierarchical, even though the same mysteries of practice, form, and art, if rightly understood, shine through all levels.

In a conclusion, I examine the connections between art and life. Here I explore the meaning of presence and place; the sacramental rituals of eating and drinking and how these are enhanced by the ceremonial use of pots made with a selfless spirit; and the often detrimental impact of modern galleries, museums, and exhibitions on the interrelationship of art and life. I emphasize the meaning brought into experience through living with pottery. In keeping with the attitude toward practice and tradition maintained throughout the book, this section concludes with a reflection on the present and future of the great tradition. In Appendix 1, I offer the reader a look at individual pots that I have loved and learned from.

The call put forth in this book, then, is toward the role the selfless practice of the traditional art of pottery can play in what I call the new age. Over thirty years ago Bernard Leach, one of my early mentors and a mediator of Japanese tradition long before I directly experienced it, wrote:

The pot is the man, he is a focal point in his race, and it in turn is held together by traditions embedded in a culture. In our day the threads have been loosened and a creative mind finds itself alone with the responsibility of discovering its own meaning and pattern out of the warp and weft of all traditions and all cultures. Without achieving integration or wholeness he cannot encompass the extended vision and extract from it a true synthesis. The quality which appears to me fundamental in all pots is *life* in one or more of its modes: inner harmony, nobility, purity, strength, breadth, and generosity, or even exquisiteness and charm. But it is one thing to make a list of virtues in man and pot and another to interpret them in the counterpoint of convex and concave, hard and soft, growth and rest, for this is the breathing of the Universal in the particular.[4]

It is to the breathing of the universal in the particular that *Zen and the Art of Pottery* pays homage, for it is in that search and in that discipline that the potter's consciousness takes wing.

ZEN AND
THE ART OF POTTERY

1

Clay as Elemental Wholeness

What is Pottery?

Pottery is the humblest of man's arts. Even before it became metaphor, pottery brought Earth to shine forth in man's world. It is best when it is most earth-honest; that includes process-honest, fire-honest, honesty of being itself. Often a beginning potter will hone a simple bowl down to where it breaks through and will learn that a pot is made of nothing— and earth. A potter's labor is consumed within the work, the craft within the art. Mere expressiveness has no depth compared with rocks and mountains, sand and sea, which speak of being and presence. Forms innovate through subtle differences of individuality within the world's infinite and pervasive roundness. The shape of nothing and of space is curved. The movement of hand and arm, head and trunk, body and mind is curved.

A cup is the sacrament of drink, a bowl the benevolent nurturance of sustenance. We have commerce with "cupping" and "bowling," not with objects at rest. But this is all too poetic unless we see the sacred as the everyday. For then again, the potter thinks not, but celebrates at every wedging; meditates on the nothingness of all forms at each centering; dies and is born again at each trial by flame. Young potters are like determined oaks; old ones like flowing willows: their works are at rest in fields and woods and beaches, and contain themselves patiently in museums. Pots play the range of the everyday-sacred, reflecting the vitality of children at play as well as the silence of a holy day. They are all. But actually, a pot's a pot: Earth come to stand as world to man.

A First View of Tradition

Through life, we are the same self. We are vaguely conscious that the time zones of childhood, middle age, and old age mesh, and that the meaning of the part is not separate from the whole of life. Similarly, our life and our meaning are not separate from the tradition in which we stand. Our common language is the readiest access to this fact. Tradition, as inherited meaning, shapes the present and portends the future, even as it accords or clashes with these. When we rebel against tradition, knowingly or not, we also fight against our own meaning— when, for example, we feel more restraint than support from our inheritance. Nevertheless, whether we affirm or deny what has shaped us, we still help to create and continue the collective dream that is tradition.

Anthropologists have said that settlements of potters within old cultures are greatly resistant to the influx of foreign influences. Literally and figuratively rooted in the earth, potters partake in a tradition as primordial as the opposition of thumb to fingers is to human evolution. It is not hard to demonstrate the evident anthropomorphism, animism, and mysticism that have persisted within the pottery tradition wherever and whenever it has existed as part of human culture. The hand itself is the earliest container. When something passes from hand to hand, we have the birth of ritual and sacrament. When a bowl or cup is freed from the human hand as a cupped hand of clay, we can take in hand or pass to another hand what the hand has freed from the hand.

Tradition, likewise, can be thought of as what is passed from hand to hand. In pottery, this is literally by "word" of hand. Moreover, history of meaning and method becomes a master, to whom we are disciples. Discipline then means to be a disciple of someone who hands down meaningful tradition. It is also in this sense that an anonymous cup made five thousand years ago can be my teacher, for the wrought clay can speak across the ages, opening up for me from the bowels of the earth the infinite forms potentially containing meaning, and the very meaning of containing itself.

One does not imitate these forms; one *participates* with them in the attitude and ritual inseparable from them. We imitate our masters only because we are not yet masters ourselves, and only because in doing so we learn the truth about what cannot be imitated.

Roundness

Modern potters often complain of roundness and symmetry, yet one might as well complain of nature or of the human form. True, roundness and symmetry are not identical, but all roundness touches somewhere on the ideal symmetry of circle and sphere, or gains its meaning in a departure from the circle.

Recently I was led to meditate on roundness from a potter's perspective. I was in my studio, where the roundness of the wheel head seemed to float above the large kicking block beneath. On the wheel head sat a new, full sphere. I thought of the sphere as an infinity of circles, or as moving circles defining a real, ideal, and virtual volume. I also saw how clay grows into these forms and how forms cannot be imposed willfully on the clay.

I also thought of the Japanese word *hara* as bodily roundness—the centering of gravity in the sphere of the belly—and of the mind as a sphere with its yin and yang. Generation itself is rounded, in that breasts and testicles and wombs swell with the spherical pressure of growth and the giving of life: out from a center. We round out our days and step within the circle of friendship. Lovers complete endless circlings of embrace. The year goes round. The womb becomes a greater sphere. One generation rounds out and a new one has found its center. We sing a round, dance a round, and drink a round.

The first form drawn by a child is often a rounded enclosure; the roundness of the eye takes in all of this. We have a home when we have drawn our loved ones and our loved things around us. If we must leave home, we make a round trip to return. In our life history, we circle the self we are, will become, and have been, in search of a center.

If value or force pulls a circling up or down, a spiral is created. If it pulls up or down toward a center, we have a vortex. A tendril is a spiral of growth. There is a family circle, and a circle of discussion. Draw a magic circle. A circle can close one out. The horizon encircles us. The infinity of the sky is a dome, the upper part of a sphere with us in the center. Science says space is curved.

A plane circles for a landing, a hawk for its prey. The wild animal goes round and round to make its bed in the tall grass. Kittens, puppies, and babies, before and after birth, curl into a ball. The porpoise takes circling leaps in and out of the ocean.

Flowers, fruits, and nuts tell the secret of center, circle, and sphere. So do droplets and snowflakes. As we age, our edges get worn off; we become round like stones rolled by the ocean or a glacier.

Presence and absence alike define roundness: the pocket in the catcher's mitt; the begging bowl; the cupped hand; the nest; the impression of the head in the pillow; the beautiful hollow between a woman's breasts, waiting for the rounded head of the beloved.

Organic thought and creation are round: We begin with the end foreshadowed and we end with the beginning. The last act of a play curves back upon the first curtain. The last brush stroke falls within the sphere set in motion by the first. Our old age rounds out our infancy, and from our infancy we can project the curve of our old age.

The theme and counter theme of music form a circle in repetition, development, and recapitulation. Despair is a whirlpool dragging us down; elation is the spiraling flight of the eagle toward the sun.

In meditating on roundness, I cannot hope to "round out" the topic here, no matter how long I engage in circumlocution. "Of all this and more," I say with a wave of my hand, "the potter's curving nothingness is full."

Centering

Centering is a quieting of motion without loss of vitality. It is a vibrant containment. Dynamic centering is never accomplished through sheer will and force. If we are off center, we virtually feel lopsided and eccentric; we cannot work unless the clay, in finding its center, centers us. In the East, a potter may meditate before throwing on the wheel. Meditation is a means of finding the mind's still center: the full nothingness through which all forms must flow toward becoming and being.

The potter carries center within, but has achieved this state only through the internalization and idealization of what he has learned through imagery and practice. The beginning potter working with a master has imagery before practice, so that it might be argued that the ideal comes first. I prefer to think that ideal and practice, like essence and existence, are both primordial and equal.

Centering is more than the quieting of a mass of spinning clay on the wheel. Properly understood, centering reveals the deeper meaning of tradition and ritual. The traditional acts of the East convey wisdom through agreed-upon conventions and rituals. The rituals are not meaningless, as mechanistic and scientific Western minds might believe them to be; rather they constitute sacraments that consecrate the mundane and the everyday. The disciple of a traditional Eastern art is working not on techniques nor even pure mastery, but on the self. It is in making oneself nothing that one is filled with the power within the tradition. The bamboo branch sings through the brush, and the spherical jar through the clay on the wheel, naturally and effortlessly.

Meditation is thus not removed from tradition as understood in the East. Even as hatha-yoga postures can be acts of meditation, the same is true of shooting an arrow from a bow or wedging and centering clay. In subtle ways, the mind negates the mind, requiring one to be a disciple of a deep tradition—to partake, in other words, of the true meaning of discipline. The true self is not the clamoring, willful ego; it is more like the Zen ideal of being totally absorbed in whatever one does, whether chopping wood or forming clay.

After thirty years of pottery, I find that I can center more and more clay on a kick wheel and use less and less speed and energy—as though a tacit knowing between my body and the clay brings us together on center. If I hurry or think ahead of myself, this dialogue falls apart.

In the West, there is the expression, "he has it all together." The East is humbler and wiser. If one knows how to center, bodily and mentally, then wherever one is there is a stillness, even if it is in the eye of the hurricane.

Wholeness

Quality and wholeness are the same because it is through the qualitative that we are aware of wholes. Parts do not *describe* the whole; rather they are instances of the pervasive quality of the whole. Thus in art there are no rules or techniques that transfer, without art, from one whole or context to another. Again, a rich and vital tradition teaches us how there can be a rule and no rule simultaneously. It leaves us with a "rule" of best practice, or an expectancy that is closest to the unexpected. This is not contradictory language. Experience itself is this kind of whole. Never what we expect, it always has its own peculiar pervasive quality. Experience and art, therefore, participate in negativity: they arise from the nothingness between one state of being and one coming into being.

Becoming, for anything that will be alive and whole, engages in a freedom not foreseen or foreseeable. One philosopher has referred to art as the free becoming of being.

Artists live in a kind of participatory and anticipatory wholeness. They are committed to the form of things unknown. Tradition shows them that these forms are natural, selfless, and timeless at the same time that they are unique, present, and part of their own destiny. Artists in the East realize that what others may consider useless and neglected are in fact essential to life. The still hub of the wheel is essential to motion, and without emptiness, the bowl cannot overflow with contents. Sculptors who are also materialists do not understand that the dark "nothingness" within a potter's forms is, in fact, the form. It has separated out a meaningful space from all possible space, and given it wholeness and quality.

Within a tradition one has the patience to be a disciple. The pervasive whole, tradition, is like the whole of one's life magnified. Standing within our life, we are also within the quality of its whole, even though it is unfinished. So it is with tradition: standing within it as a whole transcending many lives, we also stand within its unfinished wholeness. We help to determine its quality even as its quality helps to determine us. We take a share in the quality of our human condition, which is to be both contingent and free.

2

The Great Tradition

Some thinkers may say that no more is there a Great Tradition than there is a great religion—only separate traditions and separate religions. But we are on the way toward a planetary consciousness that makes this claim questionable. When I speak of the East and pottery, I draw from my experience with the Arita tradition, its details and its rituals. So what may be needed is immersion within one tradition simultaneous with liberation from it. In pottery, the West is high on liberation but low on tradition. On viewing clay pieces of Western art students, my Japanese teacher said, "Expression only; no depth." But we could as well say of much traditional art in the East: "Tradition only; no expression." Both traditions appear to be lacking.

Therefore I speak of my pottery as falling within a Great Tradition absorbing all of man's traditions of making vessel forms in clay, from earliest times to the present, East and West. At the same time, I applaud Japan's effort to keep the traditional arts free and alive, for the very meaning of tradition is in danger of being lost to modern man. One thing seems certain to me: without vital tradition man has no way of transforming the everyday into the sacred.

Why Japan?

I could turn elsewhere in the Orient to invoke the meaning of tradition in the making of pottery; however, not only do I know Japan best in this regard, but I also find represented there the most scope and continuity of this art in modern times. The old kilns and local styles—Bizen,

Tamba, Seto, Arita, Hagi—still have meaning and distinct aesthetic character. A body of forms and finishes arises around each name, and many have the continuity of a thousand years or more behind them.

Although technological advances are leveling out the differences, Japan has on the whole savored the character of place, raw material, and style intrinsic to each locale and its inhabitants. The way food is prepared and packaged, the way roofs are thatched with straw, the way grain and rice are stacked in the fields seems infinitely and beautifully varied. In much the same way, the pottery indigenous to each area has its distinctive character. In Karatsu, twenty-five kilometers from Arita, a sandy, warm-colored stoneware—not porcelain—is produced. Its characteristic glazes, decorations, and construction, involving both hand and wheel in coiling and throwing, have clear Korean influence. Among all this variety, one is hard pressed to delineate what is so clearly Japanese, yet one comes away with the impression of unity within great local diversity.

That this diversity is honored and prized is evident by the custom potters have of turning over their wheel and clay to a visiting potter, so that, by working within the style of the place, the potter can feel what is different. Yet the love of place, of what is native, of what binds life and art together through community and tradition—these are the abstract commonalities found within the differences, that comprise the embracing unity. Thus it is no surprise that where there is the most tradition there is also the most variety, without complete idiosyncracy or parochialism. Solid tradition permits the differences within and between subtraditions. The fear of repressed individuality to which Westerners attribute tradition is completely negated by an experience with Japanese ceramics.

Nonetheless, standards exist within each tradition. Not only can one easily discern an Oribe piece from a Shino or Bizen, one can also easily say, "This is a better or more typical black Oribe piece than that one." In the West, in contrast, where traditions have largely vanished, variety is diminished for lack of standards and niceties of discrimination. At the most, we discriminate among the work of individual artists: a Natzler, a Voulkos, a Robineau.

The unity behind all of the local variations found in Japanese pottery can be attributed to the pervasive influence of Zen Buddhism on Japanese traditional art in general. This special form of Buddhism was introduced to Japan in the thirteenth century; it thrived through the seventeenth century, and its "unitary cultural complex" is very much alive in the unique Japanese character today.[1] In a discussion of the influence of Zen Buddhism on Japanese art, Hisamatsu lists the following characteristics:

(1) No rule (irregular, asymmetrical)
(2) No complexity (sparse, simple)
(3) No rank (seasoned, mature, austerely sublime)
(4) No mind (natural, unstrained)
(5) No bottom (subtly profound, implying rather than nakedly expressing)
(6) No hindrance (free of attachments to things and of expectations of others or of oneself)
(7) No stirring (inwardly oriented, tranquil)[2]

Of course, the Zen tradition in art is much more than the sum of these abstract characteristics. These are merely pointers to help us articulate strands within what we already grasp as one pervasive quality in each example of Japanese pottery. They do not explain any given pot or tell us how it is made.

It is precisely such a list of qualities that I find ignored or largely unacknowledged in Western art traditions. In my own case, I found a ready response within me to Japan's pottery long before I experienced and reflected upon this Zen influence. Japan's artistic tradition, as exemplified in Zen, held out to me the promise of meaningful discipline toward the further deepening of those very qualities of clay, nature, and fire that already appealed to me. Still, there are qualities that I value as a Westerner, and these have been subtly fused with what I absorbed from the East. There is, for example, a transcendental, or vertical, Western religious outlook which seems absent from Zen's intent, but which I do not sense as inimical to a new and special unity.

The great tradition to which this book points is no syncretism, no easy unity of what may be essentially irreconcilable. Rather it holds forth the promise that beyond Zen and my Western influences there is a planetary, religio-aesthetic basis to mankind's "clay dance." Pottery has the unique capacity to invoke the archetypes of form within an idiosyncratic piece made in widely diverse cultural and historical contexts. Again, this trait is strongly represented in Japan's pottery. It is as though, in a neat reversal, form and process make the pot and potter. The potter dreams his forms in a realm of the imagination between sense and mind. West here rejoins East, for within the creative imagination it is the "formless self," "the true man of no rank"—Zen expressions— who does the work. Thus the Great Tradition may be seen to transcend Zen, or more likely, to parallel it, by plunging us into imaginal space and qualitative time—the artist's peculiar state of grace and enlightenment.

As with biological and cultural sex differences, we possess and even need to preserve and increase attributes of what we are not. As philosophers would say, we are indeed what we are not as well as what we are, for the negativity of our being has to do with what is alien. We differentiate ourselves by asserting our difference from the rest of the world, but we can subsist and expand only by appropriating what is alien.

This leads to the definition of experience itself, which always makes us wiser, though first sadder, for it never matches our expectations. As an American, I longed to experience meaningful tradition so that I could, through discipline, arrive at levels of perfection and understanding that transcend my cultural and egotistical expressive limits. A kind of temporary death is necessary for this: a giving up of self so that discipline—being a disciple within a tradition—can forge an enlarged self through its opening up toward selflessness.

It was not hard for me to give up my Western self when I studied in Japan, nor would it be hard to do so in a yoga ashram in America. In both instances, one works on the self by denying the self. But in its traditional arts Japan has kept a unity between the religious and the aesthetic that I would not find, I venture to say, in an ashram in America. The magic ingredient in the traditional arts of Japan is a blend of Zen and Shinto, the native Japanese religion. This has produced a love of nature and a "presentness" that transcend most ascetic religious disciplines I know. It might be argued that a purely ascetic religious discipline does the same. Perhaps so. But then I would have to say that the saint and the artist are different archetypes; and I would next reveal my bias by siding with Plato: beauty, which is wider than art, is more convincing than ethical action. In beauty, appearance and idea are one.

Yet, again paradoxically, we must turn to the artist, in the person of the master, to understand the route through this kind of discipleship and its relation to tradition.

Manji Inoue and the Arita Tradition of Porcelain

Over three hundred years ago, Ri Sampei, a Korean potter in Japan, discovered porcelain stone in the Izumiyama mountains, located in the small town of Arita in the southern island of Kyushu, Japan. Although the mountain is now only a picturesque shell and first-grade porcelain stone is mined a little further south in the Amakusa Islands, the discovery of porcelain clay led to the development of Japanese porcelain pottery, best known in the West through such names as Arita, Imari (the seaport from which porcelain was traditionally exported), Nabeshima, and Kakiemon (an old, established potting family, now in its fourteenth generation of porcelain production). Museums all over the world have examples of these wares. The Smithsonian, for example, has a special exhibition showing how Kakiemon designs have been imitated and adapted in French, German, Dutch, and English porcelains.

The Arita methods of throwing, shaping, decorating, and firing porcelains have their roots in Korea and China, but as with other aspects of outside culture absorbed by the Japanese, these have undergone subtle changes and developments until a distinctive Japanese manner and spirit have evolved.

My knowledge of these methods comes from three intensive work periods with the potter Manji Inoue, a master of the Arita tradition. My first contact with him was in 1967. After twenty years as a potter—working largely under the influence of such potters as Shoji Hamada and Bernard Leach who adopted the rustic mingei, or folk art style—I took a year's leave from my position at Pennsylvania State University to go to Arita and work with Manji Inoue. The second contact was in spring 1969, when Inoue Sensei, as I will call him (after the Japanese manner of using this honorific term meaning teacher) came to Pennsylvania to teach beginning and advanced courses in porcelain at the university. Finally, during the latter part of the summer of 1976, he came to America to help conclude an advanced course in porcelain throwing that, for the first time, I was attempting to teach by Arita methods.

During these twenty years of reflection upon Inoue Sensei and the methods he embodies to perfection, I have come to grasp something of the spirit and discipline of the Arita tradition. It is because I feel Western potters can learn much from Arita, and because I honor Inoue Sensei's consummate art, that I have set out to share my experience.

In the beginning, my interest in studying in Japan was not really directed toward porcelain making, of which I knew very little. Through the influence of Leach and Hamada, I was interested in the mingei movement and in the quiet, natural earlier styles of Bizen, Tamba, or Shigaraki. Nonetheless, I ended up in Arita, and it was in this lesser-known area that I came upon precision and artistry that I have not seen elsewhere in Japan or the world.

The Arita methods of clay preparation, throwing, tooling, decorating, and firing are ritualized and reveal a high level of technique. Whereas similar tools may at times be used in stoneware and porcelain pottery, once one has experienced the Arita tradition, the tools of stoneware seem sloppy and lacking in precision; and pottery tools available in America seem virtually useless if not detrimental to the art.

I was to learn all of this by entering into the master-apprentice relationship with Inoue Sensei. As in all the traditional arts of Japan, the master-apprentice relationship is a basic part of the porcelain tradition in Arita. An apprentice is chosen by the master. There is good reason for this, for once the master has chosen a *deshi* (disciple) or apprentice, he has committed himself to the important responsibility of mediating the tradition to this newest member of the potting community. Nothing is inconsequential within this relationship, whether it is learning how to make a pot, sharing tea, or sweeping up the shop. As a student of Inoue Sensei, I learned not only how to form clay; it was just as important to know how to shop for vegetables as it was to be able to distinguish a good nugget of porcelain stone from a poor one.

Without this kind of relationship in a living tradition, the initiate may never learn the single-minded and selfless commitment toward perfection that is at the heart of his art and is the essence of Japan's traditional arts. Such traditional Japanese arts as pottery have come to preserve and symbolize the way of Zen because there is a natural affinity between the artist's way and the Zen master's way.

The artist's world is one of free creation, and this can come only from intuitions directly and immediately rising from the isness of things, unhampered by senses and intellect. He creates forms and sounds out of formlessness and soundlessness. To this extent, the artist's world coincides with that of Zen.[3]

To be "unhampered by senses and intellect" is to dwell openly within the world of the creative imagination. The master of a traditional art represents this state where action and creation spring effortlessly "out of formlessness and soundlessness." Paradoxically, this state is reached when unrelenting discipline and practice have purged the rituals of the traditional art from the interference of both senses and intellect, so that the "isness" of the simplest act, such as preparing one's clay for the wheel, contains all that there is to being in the universe.

The master, thus, draws the apprentice slowly away from preconceived ideas, theories, and even history, toward life as fullness of present action. This profound lesson cannot be communicated orally, in the didactic or philosophical mode. We can know and share much more than we can say. In addition to head knowledge, there is hand knowledge, eye knowledge, and heart knowledge; and heart, eye, and hand fuse through selfless practice and example.

The master needs the student even as the student needs the master, for it is through the student's honest ignorance that the master deepens the tradition; all interpretations of the student's progress come from the living presence of the tradition as set into action by the idiosyncratic exigencies of the student. So, too, when the apprentice comes to realize the master's human frailties, he strengthens his commitment to perfection, for if the master can so strive, with all his human shortcomings, so can the apprentice. What breaks the bond is a failure of trust on the part of the apprentice, or a failure in compassion on the part of the master. But, then again, since these are not matters of logic, in Zen it is not possible either to break or maintain the bond between master and apprentice for any cause. When it is, it is. When it is not, it is not.

> There is no transference of secrets from master to disciple. Teaching is not difficult, listening is not difficult either, but what is truly difficult is to become conscious of what you have in yourself and be able to use it as your own.[4]

And this makes teaching and listening difficult indeed!

In such a master-apprentice relationship, imagery and imitation of actions and of the attitude underlying them is the chief didactic method. Imitation is only a way station, however, for it is, in itself, both impossible and even undesirable. Yet it makes possible the dialectic of question and answer between body and mind, leading toward fullness of imagery and understanding. This is a slow process, for we can never see or understand enough. I can vouch for this as a result of my own maturing process, having worked again with Inoue Sensei two years and then nine years after my initial apprenticeship; not only was I ready then to see and absorb more, but I feel that Sensei had also improved as an artist and teacher within the tradition.

Whenever I have tried to speak to Inoue Sensei about philosophical issues, he has usually answered with silence, or tapped his head and said, "Only pots in here." Apart from pottery, he remains a relatively simple person, but, then, he is rarely seen apart from pottery. Two things, apparently, first aroused his interest in me as an apprentice: I was devoted to my craft and as a potter and university professor with twenty years of experience, I was someone who could spread the Arita tradition in the West.

The precise method and sequence through which Sensei took me in my first work period with him were meant to reflect a kind of *Well-Tempered Clavier* (Bach's "training manual" for the novice harpsichordist, starting with simple compositions and moving toward increasing complexity) for the porcelain potter. The logic and clarity of this practice underlie Part 2 of this book, especially the chapters on lessons. Inoue Sensei fitted the entire range of the porcelain apprenticeship to my year in Arita, having me form ten pieces in each form along the way: straight-sided tea cup (*yunomi*), bowl, plate, lidded incense box (*kogo*), incense burner, various vases and jars, square or fluted bottles and bowls, and large vases. In addition to throwing and tooling these, I learned painting and carving techniques. The only step I was spared was the humblest one, where the novice makes up to a thousand *hamas*, or little porcelain discs on which pieces to be fired rest in the kiln.

Needless to say, in the time available, I was not able to master these forms in the way of the tradition. I still have not mastered them. Even by the master they remain unmasterable. And though I keep their purity before me, I have adapted a number of them to my Western or idiosyncratic ways, feeling no contradiction in doing so. This is not egotism. I have seen apprentices follow Sensei with a hungry and analytical eye, as though sheer mind would get them to synthesize his mastery. But the mastery is not the master's, so what analysis seeks is not even there. Sensei himself can analyze in detail—with drawings—the structural steps that attend, for example, throwing a plate off the centered mound; but that is abstraction and not technique. To think that diagramming the pose and movements of the little finger will lead anywhere is folly.

There is so much to attend to that one must look with diffused attention so that meanings on many levels, some clear and conscious, some not, may be absorbed.

In Part 2, when we come to "practical discipleship" of beginning and advanced lessons, it will be evident that, as is said in Zen, we always set to work with a "beginner's mind." We always learn as if for the first time, no matter what our stage, the meaning of tradition, centering, wholeness, roundness, style, and grace. As in a dance, the movements must feel whole and right or the form is disowned. To attempt to get there by cheating is to disdain the entire tradition. A sensitive master would walk away as though he were insulted. Sensei did just that in the middle of a class he was teaching at Pennsylvania State in the spring of 1969. A student looked up the Japanese word for "show off" and used it when Sensei was playfully making tiny sake cups with the clay remaining on his wheel. Sensei's expression changed and he stopped and left the wheel at once, without a word.

In the same vein, Sensei does not demonstrate. Whether before a huge audience or alone in his studio, whatever he makes, he makes in earnest. The discipline of a traditional art and the Zen skill of intense concentration exclude all but the skilled performance.

Sensei's own forms, though traditional, blend robustness and softness to attain a quality beautifully adapted to fired porcelain. He is a country man. He was not university educated, but spent seven years as an apprentice without pay. He represents the third generation of porcelain throwers in Arita, and, to my knowledge, has no skilled apprentice to whom he can transmit the subtle aspects of this art.

In the entire Arita area, at least in the sixties and early seventies, Sensei was making almost all of the larger and unusual porcelain shapes on commission to the other well-known studios of Arita: Kakiemon, Imaemon, and the Iwao and Koransha factories. He also made forms for his master, who was infirm with arthritis but would nonetheless decorate and sign them. Sensei did this as long as his teacher lived.

An example of the power of the knowledge and skill within the Arita tradition can be found in the large vase Sensei made for the new wing of the Imperial Palace in Tokyo. To begin with, the form was a departure from tradition. Visitors to Arita or to museums in Japan will find that large porcelain vases adhere to a limited number of forms; these are not based merely on aesthetic choice, but also on the effect that high temperatures have on large-scale porcelain pieces. Porcelain throwing is an art that must take into account the nature of the fire much more than with stoneware, for porcelain shapes actually transform during firing. A plate, for example, is bowed up in the middle when thrown because it will settle down and flatten when fired.

Because the new form of this vase was a departure, Inoue Sensei made and studied a number of smaller versions (about 35 to 40 inches high) before attempting the three large forms that he eventually created (Plate 2). Of the three, one did not survive the high fire. One is still white and undecorated after the high fire, while the third went to Kyoto, where the late Hajime Kato decorated it in overglaze gold, then sent it on to the new wing of the palace.

Inoue Sensei is now very successful in Japan. His pieces are in great demand, and they command very high prices. The Japanese have recently become avid collectors of early Japanese porcelains, as any Western collector of Arita or Imari ware will vouch; pieces have virtually disappeared from antique shops and galleries, and many pieces in the West have been bought back by the Japanese. The history of porcelain production in Japan is relatively short—less than 400 years—as compared with that of stoneware and earthenware, which reaches back into ancient times. What I have tried to do is to acquaint Western readers with this largely unknown but vital part of Japanese pottery making, and to point out also that the robust traditions of old China and Korea have found a contemporary home in Arita and in men like Inoue Sensei. Part of my mission is to see them appreciated and preserved, for the knowledge and practice they embody is largely lacking in the West and could constitute a ready basis for meaningful discipline and learning within a living tradition.

Zen

My purpose in presenting some background on Inoue Sensei and the Arita tradition of porcelain is not technical, historical, nor even purely aesthetic. Nor is it meant to center on discipleship and its discipline as ends in themselves. Rather, my aim is to point the way toward wholeness and an openness to clay and its forming as these touch on man's most poetic and sacred ties to life and nature.

Earlier I presented Hisamatsu's seven characteristics of Zen art. His list hints at terms common to Japanese aesthetics, such as *wabi* and *sabi,* which are generally not given literal definitions; rather an example or story is given to suggest their essence. Take the term *shibui,* which Hamada explained beautifully for me when he said it is "why old silver is better than new gold." In the same vein, when I invited a Japanese visitor to my American studio to select a pot to take home with him, he chose a modest, subtle one, saying: "We Japanese prefer quiet things."

According to Suzuki,[5] *wabi* is "an inexpressible quiet joy deeply hidden beneath sheer poverty," and he goes on to say that it is the art of tea, or *chanoyu,* that best expresses this idea artistically. Volumes have been written about Zen and the art of tea. It was Sen no Rikyu (1521–91) who is traditionally regarded as the founder of this art, which was brought to Japan from China in the twelfth century by a Zen monk.

On the surface, nothing could be simpler than the tea ceremony; and yet beneath the surface, nothing could be more profound. The spirit of aloneness, simplicity, and quiet pervades the atmosphere of the tea room. The room itself is humble and small, no more than ten feet square, with a low ceiling. The only decorations are in an alcove (tokonoma), where there might be a *kakemono* (hanging scroll), a vase, and usually, a single flower. An iron kettle sits on a small grate in the floor, under which there is a fire. The tea utensils are in a corner of the room, set off by a post, and the windows are covered with shōji.

Rikyu taught the samurai of his day to sit meditatively in a tearoom, sipping a cup of tea and entering into a state of quiet emptiness. Here *wabi,* that "inexpressible quiet joy deeply hidden beneath sheer poverty" could be experienced in a state transcendent but undivided.

In modern life, we in the West suffer almost unconsciously from technology's onslaught on nature, and thus have found it next to impossible to unify sense and spirit. We rarely confront a tree or stream anymore that is not held captive like an endangered species in the zoo. Hence our need for what is called "the wilderness experience." But the wildernesses too are retreating.

Japan, on the other hand, has learned to keep a delicate balance between sense and spirit in the face of nature, both inside the house and outside, no matter how small the interior or the enclosed garden. It is this refusal to allow sense and spirit to separate that I find most appealing in the Zen of pottery. This is precisely what the art of tea is all about.

Apart from such direct experiences as in a ritualized art form like *chanoyu,* one usually strives for enlightenment about Zen through a

Zen master and by taking up the path of discipleship or discipline. But
this is not always so. As in the Christian doctrine of grace, there will
always be a dispute about whether works and discipline are necessary,
or whether grace, like enlightenment, is really more of a gift. It seems
that both concepts are sound, in that the mind by its own efforts cannot
trap the deepest insights. Perhaps the clue lies in what the philosopher
Heidegger calls "meditative thinking" as opposed to the West's almost
predominant "calculating thinking." As Heidegger puts it, in meditative thinking we practice "releasement toward things" and "openness
to mystery."[6]

In the art of pottery, this means that we participate in the free becoming of "being." It is as though we could step back and yet be used
as an active agent in the creation of clay forms that, as they stand before
us, define their clear necessity to be, much as a tree, flower, fruit, or rock
does.

All the discipline and discipleship in the world would be wasted if
it did not contribute to this free becoming of being, for the fundamental
mystery of spontaneity and selfless right action are the symbols of this
spirit. It is art's meditation-in-action. Hamada could paint again and
again the same decorative strokes, yet his distinctive hand and quality
are expressively stamped on each form. The fourteenth-century Chinese
scholar Tang Hou caught this seeming contradiction:

> Set forth your heart, without reserve,
> And your brush will be inspired.
> Writing and painting serve a single aim,
> The revelation of innate character.
> Here are two companions,
> An old tree and tall bamboo,
> Metamorphosed by his unreined hand,
> Finished in an instant.
> The embodiment of a single moment
> Is the treasure of a hundred ages,
> And one feels, unrolling it, a fondness,
> As if seeing the man himself.

Admitting, then, that grace or enlightenment can fall upon the prepared or the unprepared equally, what is the purpose of discipleship
and discipline? Why study art formally? It is tempting to say that the

unprepared who see visions and make art are "natural masters." A truth lies hidden here as well, as art educators should know, for personal art and high art are not the same, but the former is essential to the deeper meaning of the latter.

To attempt to rescue the concept of discipleship and discipline in this perspective, I must set forth my simplest conceptualization of what it means to teach art. *In teaching art, the teacher engages in an interpretation of a student's self-formative process in art in relation to a common tradition.* It is because of his non-egotistical immersion in a transcendent tradition that one is a teacher or master, and it is from the viewpoint of that tradition that the teacher can perform a depth interpretation of how the student is being formed in his or her art. Neither the tradition, the interpretation, nor the student's self-formation is closed. The teacher is sensitized and rendered spontaneous in the same discipline as the student.

What makes discipleship to the way of Japanese pottery a form of esoteric religio-aesthetic practice is, of course, its connection with Zen Buddhism. Assuredly, reflection and analysis will not bring us closer to Zen. It is not even possible to do a straightforward phenomenological description of Zen's "non-thinking" stance, for to do so we would ourselves already have to dwell in that non-thinking state, and then our usual notion of description would disappear. We would have to resort to paradoxical or poetic speech tending toward (1) negation (what such non-thinking is *not*), (2) analogy (what it is *like*), or (3) injunction (what we would have to *do* to experience it).

Zen masters in the art of pottery do, in fact, instruct their students in just these ways. The instruction I received, whether verbal or non-verbal, was comprised of analogy, negation, and injunction, conveyed in actions exemplifying *Zen ki,* or Zen Activity, in my teacher's effortless choreography of the potter's actions in a Zen non-thinking state.

Often I was taught in ways that were themselves paradoxical and reminiscent of Dogen's construction: "thinking of not thinking, i.e., non-thinking." Once, for example, when I hesitated in setting down my *kanna* (metal clay finishing tool) in the exact center of the foot of a bowl to be finished on the wheel, Sensei consulted his dictionary and came up with the English expression, "Make up your mind!" This brought humor and relief to an otherwise tense situation. Sensei's injunction focused on my making up my mind to do what the mind itself cannot do, thus countering the basic behavior revealing that my mind was preventing the desired non-thinking action in the first place. In a Zen non-thinking state, I would have, through feel and repetition, brought the *kanna* on true center.

Rinzai, who founded the school of Zen bearing his name, told his followers back in the ninth century:

On your lump of red flesh there is a true person of no rank who constantly goes in and out of your mouths.[7]

In saying this, he calls us not to some transcendent reality, but to something already within us that is beyond title and surface distinctions. He also said:

In the eye, it is called seeing; in the ear, it is called hearing; in the nose, it smells odours; in the mouth, it talks; in the hand, it grasps things; in the feet, it moves.[8]

Rinzai wishes us to allow the true person of no rank to flow in and out of our sense organs by removing the obstructions that our thinking, deliberating mind imposes upon us. In like manner, Inoue Sensei repeatedly showed me the meaning of right practice in the art of pottery. In the potter, there is also a true person of no rank who constantly goes in and out of our hands, but without total immersion in selfless practice, this true person literally slips through our fingers. By working so that clay, wheel, tools, hands, feet, winter, summer, self, and mind all fuse, we put ourselves in a special qualitative time and space, which is paradoxically just *this* time and space, this *now*, when and where we may release that true person of no rank within us.

There were many parallels between my pottery apprenticeship and Eugene Herrigel's with his archery master, as recounted in *Zen in the Art of Archery*.[9] For example, when I concentrated on making the basic bowl, I learned early not to grieve over bad bowls, but it was some time before I learned not to rejoice over good ones, that it was not my "self" but the true person of no rank in me who made them. It is a lesson I still forget in my haste to take credit for and feel good about what I have done. For still another parallel with Herrigel's journey, I recall how Sensei sitting at my wheel and forming a perfect bowl with clay I had wedged seemed magically to transfer his skill to my hands when I returned to work.

In all such instances, I learned not to conceptualize, not to plan, not to evaluate, but to return to an original consciousness unbroken by thought. It is in such a state that we grasp the insight that:

> Man is a thinking reed but his great works are done when he is not calculating and thinking. "Childlikeness" has to be restored with long years of training in the art of self-forgetfulness. When this is attained, man thinks yet he does not think.[10]

In that state, man is not only like nature—the trees, the waves, the flying birds—he *is* nature.

Zen ki in art, then, is that which merges self and mind completely and forgetfully in the nature of precisely and presently what one is doing. The distance between subject and object completely disappears. The poet Basho has beautifully expressed how this may be attained in the art of painting:

> From the pine tree
> learn of the pine tree,
> And from the bamboo
> of the bamboo.

This suggests that we allow self to drop away so that we may return to things as they are in their own original nature. In this way we *become* the pine tree, we *become* the bamboo.

The modern French poet Francis Ponge exemplifies this same spirit as he "takes the side of things" in his poems and considers it a virtue "to be invaded by things."[11] As in Zen, the voice we hear when the poet writes is neither the voice of the pebble—if that happens to be his subject—nor that of the poet, but a "middle voice," the voice of poetry itself, which seems to reveal pebble and poet far more clearly than if we were fixated on one or the other. In short, subject, object, and method become intertwined as they fuse into one clear present "voice." So it is with the acts of the potter: neither the clay nor the potter nor the techniques can be singled out. Something arises which is the pure act of making. Herrigel's archery master said: "*It* shoots!" We could as well say: "*It* pots!" When we are in this state, then we have an inkling of the true person of no rank, of the formless self, of Zen in the art of pottery.

The Future of the Great Tradition

Our need for discipleship within an implicit community of work grounded on planetary tradition symbolizes a pilgrimage toward holism of body-mind. I am not urging that we bend ourselves to the traditions of old, but that we bend the traditions of old to that confluence of energies and conflicts, opportunities and frustrations, that make up our modern selves. Early followers of yoga believed that energy was centered in the belly—the *hara*—that center of gravity and force which is rooted in the earth. As time went on, these mythological energy centers moved upward, to the heart. Still later, in our time, the centering moved to the head.

Thus it is that belief is a problem with us, knowledge an insatiable desire, and feeling an indeterminate state. The Tao was centered in nature, in the belly. Thought was not separate. The body-mind thought as one and was integrated with belief and action. Life and death came like the seasons, and one laughed or became angry without vacillation or guilt.

Then an age of faith and belief arose, when man dwelled within the heart center. This is still the center in which believers, healers, integrative teachers, and artists standing in tradition must dwell if good is to flow through them. It bases itself on universal love.

But with the mind center, all changes. Action and belief become problems. We control things, try them out, distance them—and thus ourselves—from ourselves. The need for Heidegger's "meditative thinking" becomes essential. Instead of calculative thought, we must relearn "releasement toward things" and "openness to the mystery," and move away from the head to a clearing where the call of being can be heard.

For years I have facetiously said that I intended to set pottery back a good one thousand years, but by this I meant a change of heart, or a continuation of the heart and belly centers into our time—not the erection of any one standard. I like to think that if there were a nuclear holocaust a survivor who knew clay could renew the dance of making in collaboration with the elements of earth and sky, thus continuing human culture. In so doing, the belly, heart, and head centers of the body-mind could again dream of equilibrium. As an art educator, a teacher of pottery, a potter, and a theorist of education through art, I must see at close range and from afar, simultaneously, in all that I mediate from within the Great Tradition. My aim is not just the potter, or even the good pot, but achievement of body-mind holism through participation in discipleship within the Great Tradition. The *I Ching* says:

All that is visible must grow beyond itself, extend into the realm of the invisible. Thereby it receives its true consecration and clarity and takes firm root in the cosmic order.

In actuality, I would like to show how the simple basic bowl can "take firm root in the cosmic order." This I cannot teach directly. I can only recover this truth again and again, in this small bowl, here and now. I can contain the ocean and the spirit in cupped hands of clay.

The trees planted around my studio grow up to dwarf it, and the roof of my shed ages. These give a unity, with continuity, and deepen presence of place through the very vicissitudes of age and change.

As pottery is a daily pursuit to which I go eagerly, and as I see more clearly what it is and can be and what it is not and probably cannot be, I tend to forget that there are many people who do not know it that way at all. Purely professional teachers, therapists, or other practitioners, faced with the overwhelming urgencies of the educational and human dialogue, may have little feel for pottery as a discipline. I like to feel, however, that insofar as men and women become whole by becoming completely subservient to their discipline, to that extent they come to a humility and reflexive insight which at least borders on wisdom.

Wholeness of body-mind is hard to achieve. It's not accomplished by a mere act of will or by taking another person's work as a standard; it comes out of the tapestry one has been working on (in the quiet, and often in the dark). It helps to have worked hard, to have worked with someone else who is productive over a period of time, and to have experienced a tradition directly.

This book celebrates a turning from the heart toward wholeness. Zen in the art of pottery is no more nor less than centering the body-mind by dwelling with a beginner's mind in the heart of the simplest act. It is a meditation in action in which the humblest bowl and the largest sphere arise from the same deep peace, where one's best forms and decorations seem no longer one's own but appear as though uninvited, from out of a state of grace; and where one has learned to let the noise and press of institution, gallery, and fame itself merge into the sound of wind and rain, the feel of sun and morning fog.

"Right practice is already enlightenment." One pots no differently after enlightenment (if we are even permitted to know what and when that is), but merely digs clay, wedges, centers, forms, tools, decorates, fires, and places jars here and there, in solitude or in a community. *"Il faut toujours travailler"*—"One must always be working," said Rodin. But even this idea must not be held tightly like an inviolable rule. The French also say of a newly plowed but unplanted field, *"C'est de la terre en repos"*—"It is earth resting." We must, as well, with Whitman, "loaf and invite the soul." Pots are made at the seashore and in the mountains, both high and low, ecstatic and sorrowful, at the wheel and deep in the fields of summer.

So, as a Westerner seeking to be East and West of the Great Tradition, I intuit that even Zen is parochial. It is the pure spirit that must express itself in holding the *oshibera, kanna,* brush, or body-mind a certain way—not just habit, ritual, or tradition, narrowly conceived.

All the tales of the spirit, all the tales of love, all the tales of art are the same. We are being itself through spirit, love, and art; and each of these is in all, and all of these are in each.

The simple art of pottery bridges that silent space where the natural, the human, and the divine appear to the initiate who sees pottery as a way, as an esoteric spiritual discipline: East and West of the Great Tradition.

3

The Community of Work

The Basis for Community

There is good reason why artistic learning takes place in some kind of genuine community or, in its absence, in some kind of internalization thereof. The artist's world view is an ideal one, yielding the faith that fragments will at last come together, whatever their history of conflict on the way. Artists live in a kind of participatory and anticipatory wholeness. The artist's life is not founded on the idealist side, however, as much as it is on the progressive actions that qualitatively lead imagination's encounter with feeling toward expression.

Such an orientation presents severe problems in learning—so much so that I have argued that art must again and again be learned all at once, and thus cannot be "taught" at all. Nevertheless, paradoxically, it is indeed learned—either in a context where there is a master-as-teacher or where there is a coming-to-mastery without a teacher. To work effectively, both of these contexts occur within community. By *community,* I mean a setting where open dialogue and communion pervade all relationships. Without the binding power of genuine community, the faith to treat fragments of feeling and experience as meaningful and pregnant toward form is stifled.

Within the Great Tradition stand countless famous and anonymous souls, living and dead, who are my peers and friends. The ideal of community, of common work within a tradition or toward a common goal, always haunts the shadows of the studio and lingers within the working clutter of the kiln.

An organically unified working farm has about it a similar camaraderie, wholistically seen and experienced, through productive labor and the cycles of nature. In Japan, wherever a potter's compound survives, there is an ordered human and natural hierarchy to processes and labors, welded together through respect for tradition and role. This applies even to the most common laborer, who is often able to function with a grace not seen in the highest places. One member of the community may only split the red pine for the kiln, but that job is as essential to the whole operation as fashioning and decorating the most exquisite piece.

The pottery cycle itself is a microcosm of man-nature-culture. From digging clay to forming it into wares, to glazing and firing and distributing them, the flow of energy from stage to stage is akin to that ordered by the seasons for the farmer. This irreversible cycle is in itself a ground for community, for it overpowers the individual will toward the common good. Even a lonely potter, like a farmer working alone, feels this kinship with unseen coworkers.

At various points in my life, I have engaged in a pottery partnership, either by taking on apprentices or becoming an apprentice myself, and I have also found the sense of community arising spontaneously in my classes as I set out to teach porcelain, the making of large pots, or the building and firing of a wood-fire kiln.

When we participate in a community undertaking, nature and culture aid us in exceeding our limits as humans, allowing the mythic and heroic dimensions of existence to appear. This is why, in my view, there is always a religious flavor to the experience of community. We are transcended and transformed on every side. The mythic becomes the real, and we are half-gods, half-men. All of this happens when, as Martin Buber points out, dialogue occurs between the participants.[1]

As unfinished selves and beings, we are ideally suited to lose ourselves in the pursuit of what we are not. It is as though our finite shadows are thrown by an infinite source. The subject, game, or play toward which we turn does not respect us, but has its own drive to become fully realized. All community is an expanded state based on the synergy of multi-dimensioned dialogues with a common core. Each true dialogue, where the limits of the partners are exceeded in their pursuit of something coming into true being, already evokes the full notion of community. In this sense, lovers are a community, for the care that exists between them evokes the myth of ever-expanding and ready-to-be-realized potential inspired by what is "other." Artists are likewise a community, for out of their receptive meditative state they prepare themselves to be addressed by that which, springing from nothingness, now through them has a nascent being.

Common Labor and Work

Labor, according to Hannah Arendt, is self-consuming, leaving no traces, but it is always honorable, for it sustains life.[2] The preparation of meals, the tilling of the soil, the cleaning of home and studio, are examples of such activities. Work, on the other hand, persists in time, adding to the durability of life. Traces are left behind. Labor is thus transformed as it is absorbed into work.

In pottery, work rests upon a foundation of labor. Those who disdain the labor or approach it with the wrong spirit, undercut their work. Tradition reinforces right attitude; respect for sweeping up the studio or caring properly for the clay is prized over an aristocratic bearing that considers humble labor demeaning.

For example, one could hardly be called a potter, in the traditional sense, if he bought ready-made clays and glazes, and hired someone to fire his pieces. True, in Japan, common laborers may perform some of the tasks required in a pottery village or compound, because a symbiotic division of labor has been set up. But the ideal is to retain sensitivity for all details of the process, and this requires bonding in common labor and work.

Special Communal Work

How can I write now about instances of community that I have experienced as a potter and teacher? These reverberative networks of holism—standing outside time—are ineffable by definition. Intelligent mystics keep silent and let the story be read through their lives, or by an intuitive disciple, or not at all. In a very real sense, it doesn't matter beyond itself.

At most I could present readers with testimonials, but these are notoriously unconvincing to those not already convinced. Belief is not a state that can be forced on anyone. On the other hand, what is whole pervades one's thinking, leading to elaborations that are not the flame but nonetheless come into view through its sources of light. So, why not cast a few shadows? I cannot say how it will be, or even should be, but I can examine the texture, if not directly the quality, of what was.

My instances of community I will limit here to two. In the first, I took a group of graduate students in pottery to a studio in the woods, and there we committed ourselves to a communal venture.

We began by digging native stoneware clay and preparing it for the wheel. In an age when everything is a packaged commodity that money can buy, digging and preparing a local clay can be a purifying and unifying act. Clay-digging expeditions with students and fellow potters are like celebrations and meaningful rituals. The digging, sorting, checking, bagging, and carrying are activities enjoyed most when shared. Concern for nature and ecology dictates how clay should be removed and how the land should be left; individual potters are not the ravagers that clay mine companies are, but their rights to land will be equally questioned. When I remove clay from state lands, for instance, I make only shallow holes, then refill them with earth and fallen branches, so no scars are left behind.

In any case, assuming permission to dig has been granted, and care and concern for the environment are evident, this shared labor leads to the acquisition of a clay with characteristics quite unlike any other. The kind of pottery formed in a particular locale is tied directly to indigenous materials and resources. Re-establishing this tie, when it has been lost, does much toward renewing one's desire for the continuity and newness of a living tradition. The ideal or the possibility of a self-sufficient pottery community is easily kindled by such activities.

Once my community of students and I had thus prepared the clay for the wheel, we set to work collaboratively and anonymously: no piece was to have individual ownership, and several potters could work on one piece at various stages. Nothing was signed. It was as important to clear a space or clean up an area as it was to form or decorate a piece.

We had four or five wheels for throwing, but we also pinched and formed many pieces by hand. At the start, we used primitive firing methods—sawdust kilns and wood-fired raku.

My memory does not preserve numerous details from this summer class, which expanded far beyond the official boundaries of "class." I do remember waking at dawn one morning to the sound of a bamboo flute. The wood fire for the kiln had been started, and three dim figures could be seen dancing around the kiln. I also recall that some participants were not ready for this communal venture, bringing in attitudes and vibrations that did not fit. But, on the whole, the majority of the students and I were happy to drop pretenses, self-importance, and feelings of competition and to enter into a complete collaboration: The pot that I threw, someone else tooled, and still another decorated. No ideas were stolen or protected, for they belonged to the group as a whole.

When the days of our community came to an end, we had to decide what to do with works we had made. Should we bury them, give them away, sell them for some cause? We decided to keep them as tangible reminders of an unusual experience, and we used a random lottery system, so that no one person would get first choice in any consecutive rounds. A certain communal fairness of acquisition of value pervaded even the lottery system, for no one chose more value or spirit than he felt was reasonable.

A summer or two later, again an advanced pottery class and I took up a communal commitment. This time, our goal was to build a simple version of a Japanese climbing hill kiln, or *noborigama,* to be fired in the old Bizen, Tamba, and Shigaraki manner, with wood alone, pots unglazed except by the fly-ash from the fire itself.

We were given permission to use a hill slope six miles from town for our kiln, which was to be a kind of Tamba-inspired tube or trench kiln, half underground, sloping up a hill, with fire box on one end and chimney on the other. The kiln chamber would have no doors; instead, the roof would be put into place after loading and removed after firing.

The focus for this kiln-building was mentally and physically much clearer than the idea of anonymous collaboration. A genuine community spirit—as pure as I have known—arose, and demanded of us all a spirit of work and giving in keeping with the wholeness of each person. Each one did what could be done. There was no mention of grades, and there were no work factions or leadership crises.

The community of labor and work begun by digging clay and building a kiln was extended into collecting, splitting, drying, and stacking huge quantities of red pine wood. Here was an effort impossible without many devoted hands, and all that effort paid off visibly in terms of a transformed environment. What had been a grassy hill slope was turning into a potters' compound or settlement. Tents were pitched, and the kiln was surrounded by tall racks of split pine.

An incidental benefit from the camaraderie of common labor and work was that of the appreciation of the quality of the life-world of each person participating. Eating and working and sweating and resting together became the ground for much unhurried and unforced sharing. I question whether this could happen in a retreat or encounter weekend or Esalen intensive.

I have no more than touched on community, this most mysterious of topics. I could have alluded to other cases of community, such as when I taught the making of large pots, or porcelain according to the Arita tradition. But these few will do for now. Community arises from a common ground of tradition, but it is not limited to the content or goal chosen by any specific group. There is, however, always a common goal or content in instances of community, just as there is in dialogue. In both, we gain our true selves, our becoming selves, as we lose ourselves in the "play" of some truth that is coming to stand in the world.

The Mythic: Kiln Gods, Absolute Forms, and Clay Presences

In a chapter on community, I feel drawn toward that place in experience where new sacraments and rituals come into being. Revelation and divination and possession have in common the idea that the divine has penetrated the human or been penetrated by it.

Writers have spoken of myth as that which takes over in the night spaces of the mind. It is as though there is a native or folk wisdom more bred in the bone marrow than in the brain. Archetypes permeate our dreams and our relationship to nature, both within and outside our body-minds. In a time of the breaking of myths, they become even more important. Our loss of innocence in the sphere of belief presses upon us as moderns. We long to stand alone before the ocean or in a virgin forest. We long to stand together in unreserved love.

The community of work in pottery under the Great Tradition stimulates these less than conscious mythogenic forces. Before the elemental wholeness evoked by clay work, we feel the need to participate in the unity of what Heidegger calls the four-fold: we stand between sky and earth, between gods and men, as though we ourselves were the subject matter of a dialogue between these elemental forces.

It is therefore healthful to pick up a piece of clay to fashion a "kiln god" as a supplication or collaboration with the unknown forces of fire. My students and I usually crowd the projection of the kiln door arch with new kiln gods before each firing. Those from the previous firing go inside the kiln, beneath the floor, to be high fired. Then later they take their place in the collection of used, but not impotent, kiln gods encircling the high areas of the wooden kiln shed.

Kiln gods are made without preconception and stand outside aesthetic criticism. Through searching fingers, at work according to an ancient urge, kiln gods clean out the mind. They deploy our technological need to control the fire and remind us of divine intervention in every important enterprise. They make it unlikely that we will hurry the fire or think small thoughts during the firing.

Many times I have seen insensitivity and a lack of humility "punished" by a kiln firing. When potters think they know it all, unpredictable forces collect to knock them down—or so it seems. The spirit, the attitude, the "vibrations" do affect our world, our potential community, and our work.

The quiet "absolute" forms of pots made within the Great Tradition usher in another dimension of spirit. The forms seem not quite ours, yet they are not cast in a predetermined mold, for the absolute in art exists only as presence, as the incarnation and yet the source of our desire. It convinces us, as Plato knew, much more than the grandest ethical action (hence the artist cannot be replaced by the saint).

So what we do in decoration and in firing is not undertaken lightly. It has all the seriousness of divine play. The "game" of throwing, tooling, decorating, glazing, and firing takes over and forms us, or transforms us, more than we do it. Some of the simplest and purest shapes in pottery are almost like visual meditations. We search their contours and volumes in quietness of mind, and blessed by the sensitive decorations of hand and fire and formative processes, they become inexhaustible qualitative wholes. The anthropomorphism of these forms is also apparent: lips, mouths, shoulders, necks, bellies, feet, ears, arms. A fused physiognomy results, a character unique to the piece.

At various times in my years as a potter, certain hieratic and primitive "clay presences" have evolved (Plates 3, 4). These have much in common with kiln gods, but they can be more sustained, more dreamlike. Often they are primal mothers and valley spirits, personifications of the feminine, of the fecund mystery of life continuity and of unbroken spiritual lineage. At still other times, they are personifications of nature: the river spirit, the tree of life, the ocean, the mountain, and the arc of the sky. These can fuse into a complete environment or landscape, a universe of the universal.

As a wheel potter, one learns the structure of forms in clay, so that expression and formation are always one, neither clay nor idea running ahead of oneself. I prefer to work from a "clay bank," in which scores of pre-thrown cylinders, cones, spheres, necks, cross sections, and the like are kept in a damp state, ready to be joined, cut, fitted, and shaped. Thus one can improvise without delay, taking what is ready and waiting as both stimulus and response to the mythic dream of a clay presence.

When I walk through a museum and see how this mythogenic spirit has expressed itself throughout history, I feel an unbroken brotherhood in clay, in which I am usually the youngest son. There is so much to learn without any need for imitation. And all of this speaks to deep and unsatisfied needs within us.

1. Izumiyama in Arita, Japan, the mountain where Ri Sampei discovered porcelain stone about 350 years ago. Most of the mountain has been mined for porcelain and glaze material.

2. Manji Inoue at work (1967) on a large lidded jar for the new Imperial Palace in Tokyo.

3. Three Hieratic Figures. Stoneware, assembled from thrown pieces; slips, ash glaze. By the author. H. 4–9½ in. (10.1–24 cm.).

4. Six Hieratic Figures. Stoneware, assembled from thrown pieces; various slips, ash glaze and salt glaze. By the author. H. 7–15½ in. (17.7–38.7 cm.).

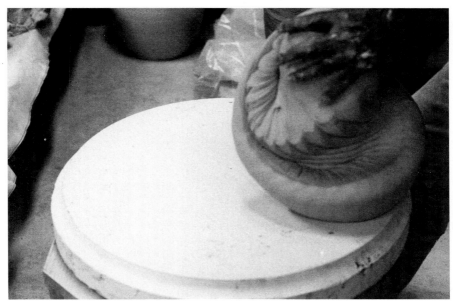

5. Manji Inoue wedging porcelain clay, showing the rhythmical "petals" that form as the clay turns.

6. Examples of bisque tooling chucks.

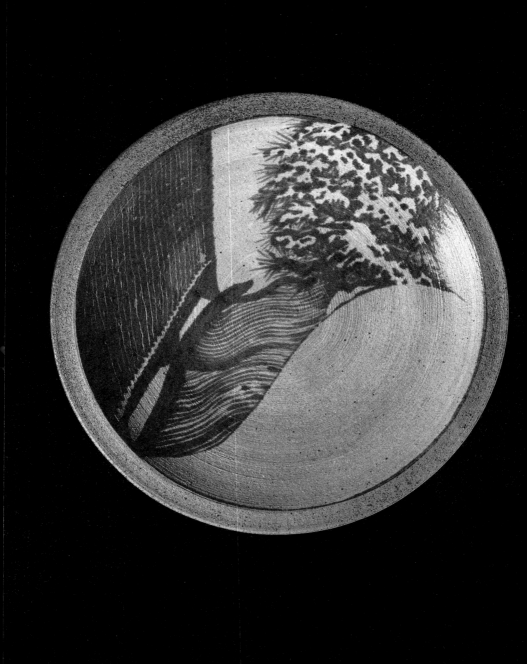

7. Winter Sun Screen Plate. Stoneware; white and black slips, ash glaze with overspray. By the author. D. 17¼ in. (43.7 cm.). Coll: Dr. Joan Novosel-Beittel.

8, 9. The author working on a tall cylinder by coiling and throwing; finishing a large jar formed from two hemispheres, which were extended by adding thrown coils in the middle section.

10. Gathering of the Ancients. Jar, stoneware, thrown, coiled, pinched with a stamp; stains, ash glaze, and over-sprays. By the author. H. 22 in. (55.8 cm.).

11. Earthenware jar. Japanese, Jomon period,
c. 3000 B.C. H. 8¼ in. (21 cm.). Coll: Museum
of Art, The Pennsylvania State University.

12. Two stoneware incense boxes. Japanese, Shoji Hamada and Kanjiro Kawai, c. 1965–67. Hamada, H. 2⅛ in. (5.4 cm.); Kawai, H. 2 in. (5.2 cm.). Coll: the author.

13. Two black stoneware spheres. American, Lawrence Jordan, 1979. H. 7¾ in. (19.7 cm.) and 10¾ in. (27.3 cm.). Coll: the author and Dr. Joan Novosel-Beittel.

14. Hexagonal porcelain vase. Japanese, Masashi Sakaida (Kakiemon XIII), c. 1967, Arita. H. 9$\frac{5}{8}$ in. (24.5 cm.). Coll: Museum of Art, The Pennsylvania State University.

15. Trees on Winter Fields. Jar, stoneware; white slip *hakeme*, painting in black slip, ash glaze with oversprays. By the author. H. 15$\frac{1}{2}$ in. (39.9 cm.). Coll: Museum of Art, The Pennsylvania State University.

16. Winter Flock Vase. Native stoneware; white and black slip, ash glaze with overspray. By the author. H. 6¾ in. (17.1 cm.). Coll: Saga Museum of Porcelain and Ceramic Arts, Arita, Japan.

17. Salt-glazed rectangular bottle. Japanese, Shoji Hamada, c. 1967. Stoneware. H. 7¾ in. (19.6 cm.). Coll: the author.

18. Bowl, Japanese, Shoji Hamada, c. 1963. Stoneware. D. 7⅛ in. (18.1 cm.). Coll: the author.

19. Jar of the Summer Fog. Stoneware; white slip *hakeme*, painting in various slips, oversprays, ash glaze, copper blush. By the author. H. 13 in. (33 cm.). Coll: Dr. Yasuro Kamachi, Arita, Japan.

20. Homage to Hokusai. Stoneware; white slip, wax resist with ash glaze, black stain with overspray. By the author. H. 8¼ in. (21 cm.). Coll: Masashi Sakaida (Kakiemon XIII), Arita, Japan.

21. Using a *dami-fude* (large brush) to float underglaze blue (*gosu*) onto bisque porcelain, at the Kakiemon studio in Arita.

22. Snow Pine Jar. Stoneware; white slip with resist and black slip painting, iron stain, ash glaze with oversprays. By the author. H. 18⅜ in. (46.7 cm.). Coll: Saga Museum of Porcelain and Ceramic Arts, Arita, Japan.

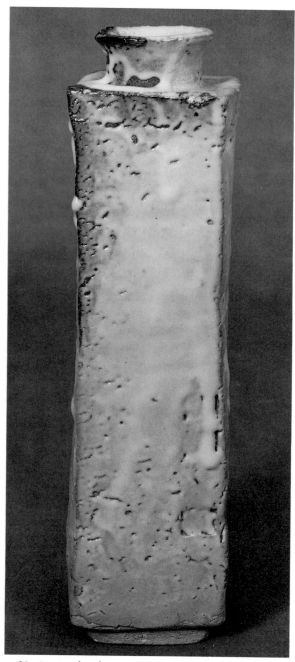

23. Square bottle. Japanese, Kyusetsu Miwa, Hagi,
c. 1967. Stoneware. H. 11 in. (28 cm.). Coll: Museum
of Art, The Pennsylvania State University.

24. River Landscape Vase. Porcelain; decoration scratched through underglaze blue, clear glaze. Made by the author in Japan at the workshop of Manji Inoue. H. 8 in. (20.3 cm.). Coll: Dr. Joan Novosel-Beittel.

25. Lidded box. Stoneware; carving through black slip, ash glaze. By the author. H. 2⅛ in. (5.4 cm.). Coll: Yasuo Ishii, Fukuoka, Japan.

26. High-footed ceremonial bowl. Native stoneware, carved; white and black slip, copper red and
ash glazes. By the author. H. 3½ in. (8.9 cm.).
Coll: Shigeharu Ito, Fukuoka, Japan.

27. Footed bowl. Native stoneware, stamped, thrown,
and pinched; ash glaze. By the author. D. 6 in. (15.2
cm.). Otsubo Collection, Fukuoka, Japan.

28. Cup with handle. Native stoneware; white and black slip, ash glaze. By the author. H. 3 in. (7.6 cm.).

29. Wine cup. Native stoneware; resist with black slip, ash and celadon glazes. By the author. H. 2 in. (5 cm.).

4

Holistic Participation of The Body-Mind

The Concept of Body-Mind

Perhaps the concept of body-mind is Western, in the sense that in the East it has never been assumed that body and mind are separate. The dividing, calculating, controlling, reasoning mind can easily cross a line beyond which it forgets that the head merely sits on top of a body of which it is a part, and which often functions without the mind's interference.

Western science and reasoning have reinforced this division by establishing laws that on the surface may seem to enhance nature, but actually destroy it. That other "reality" that comprises our everyday experience is of a different order and consigned to a subjective and private sphere. On the scientific side, the body is secondary, although paradoxically it must supply the reading of nature that confirms the primary evidence on which reason rests. Mechanism—the theory that life can be explained in terms of physics and chemistry—or, more narrowly, positivism—which bases knowledge solely on data of sense experience—forces our experiential world into pleasure-pain cycles because of the body-mind split it engenders, for as we advance the mind toward pleasure in the subjective sphere, we inevitably seem to pay a price within the impersonal, objective sphere.

Yet in watching children or animals, dancers or athletes, we catch glimpses of the indisputable fact that body and mind are primordially not two but one. We prefer a doctor who treats us as persons—not as bodies that are diseased. We have come to accept the interaction of body and mind, or psyche and soma; witness the growing number of advocates of holistic health and holistic medicine, where disease is not separated from attitude, life experiences and one's daily regime. Even chronic and incurable illnesses have been shown to respond to and reverse their trend under autogenic instruction, guided imagery, and environmental and attitudinal change.

Through biofeedback, so-called involuntary processes can be influenced by mental participation under some integrative discipline. The body-mind learns to reestablish its lost oneness, realizing that the mind is capable of being both healer and slayer. The slaying part is often an unconscious, unwitting participant, at times part of the repressive influence of the culture itself. A famous anthropologist conjectures that aging is a process that is partially induced. People think "old thoughts" about themselves that are insidiously reinforced by their cultures. Instead of dancing, they settle into an aged shuffle. Because they can no longer play football or climb mountains, they do nothing physical, or they passively watch the active exploits of others on television.

The same separation of body-mind affects our diets. If we are unhappy or dissatisfied, unloved or unloving, we turn to food, drink, or drugs. To stimulate our lethargic bodies in the morning, we take an "upper" with coffee and, later on, to quiet down, a "downer" with alcohol. We increasingly ingest meals at fast-food places where all is prepackaged and identical, ready to eat in seconds.

When the body-mind is one and at rest, however, in quiet and pleasant surroundings, eating and drinking become rituals and the food itself a sacrament. Steamed fresh vegetables, a piece of ripened fruit, a few nuts—these become satisfying celebrations of life and make us thankful for the beauty and nourishment of what is simple, whole, and pure. Then our dependence on nature and our harmony with it take precedence over our control of it. When such thoughts nourish us, the food is nourishing.

When body and mind go their separate ways, we suffer the effects of this divorce. The body retains traces of trauma and division; one's history does indeed become carved into flesh.

We were all meant to be ideal body-minds, but, alas! The miser can scarcely be envisioned as a smiling dancer, lithe and free. Instead we conjure up a fitting face and posture. In more idiosyncratic ways, and in addition to our genes, we write our histories in our body-mind. Ken

Dychtwald, for example, has given convincing "readouts" of a person's history and life attitudes by carefully watching the way he walks, sits, stands, and responds to a push from the front or back.

But, again, these conditions are plastic and reversible as long as one lives. What has been miseducated and divided can be reeducated and united. In fact, our very idea of wholeness seems to come from nature and from those times when we felt in harmony with it. Love and art and play and devotion conjure up the body-mind as unified and timeless.

Disciplines for Body-Mind Unity

The East provides rich regimes of practical discipleship, or discipline, toward unifying the body-mind. It is because of the existence of traditions such as those in the East that we can turn to accumulated wisdom for our guidance. These traditions are not *essential* to body-mind wholeness, but they represent a journey back to where we all started—with unified body-minds. And when we eventually return home from such a journey, we have the richness of our travels within us, so that home itself is thereby transformed.

In addition, the concepts of meditation, biofeedback, autogenic instruction, and the like suggest a subtlety and split within the mind itself. It is at this point that the dialectic of a holistic participation of body-mind comes forth. East and West themselves constitute a dialectic—the West with its concentration on a split-off mind opposed by the East with its concentration on no-mind. The full dialectic is being—nothing—becoming. The West overstresses being, the East nothingness. By stressing the conflicting aspect of the movement—nothingness—the East has been able to preserve traditions for disciplining the body-mind toward becoming. As I earlier indicated, through art, love, play, and devotion, we give up ourselves and become what we are not. If we were able to experience these deeply and continuously, we would cheat death, for we would dwell timelessly within the wholeness of perpetual becoming. We would know only the qualitative immediate present, as pure creation or infinity. But we are finite. Hence the necessary discipline of nothingness so that we may be visited by the movement toward wholeness. Unity is achievable momentarily. Neither wholeness nor unity is a continuing state. The greatest master may be more endowed with these qualities, but if he makes claims beyond that, he suffers from what Jung calls "inflation"—the belief in over-determination of one's own spirit.

It is because of our contradictory nature that we must do the "work" of the spirit. When we practice hatha yoga, for example, we try to unify opposed forces in the body (literally translated, "hatha yoga" means joining the energies of the sun and the moon). If we take up *aikido*, we travel the road toward "the meeting of spirit"—again, a literal translation. The Genesis myth has wholeness preceding the fall, and from then on it is a problem of rediscovering wholeness. This may be a mythological way of saying that the split within us must perpetually be transcended and healed.

Willing alone will not take us there. In *Awareness through Movement*, Moshe Feldenkrais effectively demonstrated that direct will distorts the body; it is only through subtle disciplines of movement that the body can be freed and the mind educated toward increased awareness and integration. Thus, in a Western innovation, he uses the mind indirectly so that it can be enlarged and reintegrated with the body.

It is as though there is an external and an internal or subtle self. Exemplification of this phenomenon may be found in the accounts of Eugene Herrigel's *Zen in the Art of Archery,* Michael Murphy's *Golf in the Kingdom,* and Timothy W. Gallwey's *The Inner Game of Tennis.* The latter two, more Western in their view, assume an actual split into an outer and inner self. The inner self is intuitive and feeling, risking, playful, immediate and qualitative. It is opposed by a critical, realistic, mediating, purposeful, calculating outer self. The trick seems to be to have the outer self command the inner self to take over. It is indeed a trick on the calculating outer self to use its will against its will, just as the meaningless mantra willfully used in meditation knocks the mind's restless willing.

In the West, a kind of sorcerer, magician, anti-hero—like Don Juan in Castenada's accounts, or Shimas Irons in Michael Murphy's book—appears mysteriously to lead the way toward discipleship. There is no coherent tradition available, but instead wisdom is amassed and developed by a charismatic, sectarian guru. The East seems more centered, for tradition and master or guru have congruence, lineage, and pedigree. Yet the end is the same. Neither technique nor method will suffice. A change of heart and will are implied within a journey of discipleship. Ascending stages of the way are set forth, but each implicates the whole tradition.

As sophisticated moderns we are apt to think that only primitive or naive minds take tradition seriously. And, indeed, our problem may be that of listening, of finding the word spoken by tradition across the present, from past to future. It can be said that in tradition we pass from naive to knowledgeable understanding through an arc. The center of the arc is practice, imitation, explanation. Discipline is rooted in wholeness, but it is mediated. Understanding is immediate. Explanation and understanding, imitation and internalization, outer and inner body are the dialectics of this arc. And arc by arc we round out the snake that swallows its tail—the symbol for eternity itself.

What is meditation? What is wholeness? What is holistic participation of the body-mind, both in general, and in pottery particularly? The enlightenment of Zen Buddhism has it that chopping wood and wedging clay are the same. When we are in love, are caught up in music, dance, or write a poem, we have no reason to meditate, as though it were only one kind of activity. Holistic participation of the body-mind, centering, meditating are all one. The trick is to use no tricks and be utterly present-minded in whatever we do.

Body-Mind in Pottery

Pottery is a proper microcosm of world and life for our meditation as action. Within the perspective of the Great Tradition, there is indeed an *inner game of potting;* there is indeed *deep play as flow.* The inner, intuitive self, the *luminous body,* takes over from the willful, calculating self.

When I wedge clay or center it on the wheel with this attitude, my body-mind is participating holistically. I am not at deep rest with awareness, but in full action with awareness. Both are meditation. I cannot claim more for pottery than anything else we might do in this spirit, but along the path of self-formation within the Great Tradition, there are ideal opportunities for this meditative transcendent transformation, this Zen of the simple act. To pride oneself on doing away with tradition in pottery, then, would be to deprive oneself of a deeply meaningful discipleship. The very repetition of the acts, the symmetry and centeredness, the timeless echoes of form and fire, all of these symbolize getting somewhere by going nowhere, by being truly and wholly present in this humblest and most speechless art.

Imagery can help while we learn these lessons of holistic participation. We have a feeling self as well as a directing self. We can listen to our body-mind. Often I will take a student's hands to ensure that a movement is felt, not just seen. I urge students to pay attention to their breathing, or to stop chewing gum, or to forget that their foot is kicking the wheel. I do not allow a radio in the studio. I tell them, "Clay is your medium," or, "Imagine a sturdy steel rod in the center of the clay and lean on it." Again and again I have them watch an entire movement, then practice it, then watch again, and so on.

Soon they will be able to ask questions—"Why is it that I get this inverted, fat lip when I open up the ball?" Or, "Why does the bottling tool dig up the bottom of my bottle?"—and at that point it is easy to round out the actions that need to accompany the image.

Tacit knowing, according to Michael Polanyi, occurs when through our body-mind we "know more than we can tell." As the blind man reads the world through his cane, so do we as potters read the world through the vibrations in our hands. We take the world into our body, and our body into the world. So with a bottling tool, the nerves reach to the tip of the stick and we "see" from within the dark interior of the expanding sphere. I find that as the curve of a sphere swells from within, and as I trace and have dialogue with that thrust through my outside hand, my entire body responds with an effortless exhalation which settles with the ripening thrust of the curve. In such action, knowledge dwells within the body-mind.

It takes years before teachers learn to find equivalent words for their actions. So it is that the student will not be able to say in words what he or she has done. My best students may imitate me for several years, and in so doing, show me what is worthy of imitation, leading me to improved integration by their very example. Curiously, the ideal exists even in the crudest holistic effort. Also, students will sometimes carry further than I something I have set in motion for their benefit, thus teaching me where a certain development needs to go.

There are many ways in which traditional pottery can keep one centered and whole. I consider it very important to my sanity and balance that the art I practice is pottery. Its continuity over time and a variety of activities lays a unifying web over divisiveness. The pot I threw on a Sunday in January from clay I dug in October may be decorated in March and fired in June. It is part of a series of such extended time unities. It defines its own qualitative time, canceling out the university schedule, committee meetings, interviews, exhibitions, and public lectures. What I have been able to learn about patience, conservation of energy, and completeness of participation in my years as a potter stands me in good stead for my participation in my other professional commitments.

The stages of this art symbolize the dispersion, newness, and goal-consciousness we feel on an enjoyable journey. Since individual pieces are always at varied stages, it is as though a hundred spontaneous side excursions occur along the way. Holistic participation of the body-mind, then, means this dispersion, this gathering of many fragments into one unity, just as much as it means the fullness of each present act as it rises and falls within time. The parts of pottery symbolize this journey, just as the series of pots symbolize the superordinate myth that floats above one's life in works.

5

Beginning Lessons

I know of no better way to introduce beginning lessons than to share the handout I currently give my students on their first day in my class. Of course, beginners need not restrict their introduction to pottery to ten weeks, as this course does; but I feel that the curriculum I follow for Beginning Ceramics will give readers a good overview.

Beginning Ceramics

Content: This course will concentrate on wheel-throwing as a discipline of the self in relation to clay—"claying." The methods that will be described, demonstrated, and taught are based largely on the tradition of Japanese ceramics. The aim of this course is to make the basic hand and body motions so habitual that sensitivity and spontaneity are natural byproducts.

After throwing, we will progress to tooling, finishing, decorating, bisquing, and glazing. We will be using mostly stoneware (clay that matures or becomes vitreous at 2300° F and above).

We will make our own tools, but students should buy their own potter's needle (a dissecting needle set in wood), a small piece of chamois leather, a small natural sponge, and brushes for decorating (Japanese-style brushes with long soft hair are best).

Attitude and Requirements: The beginning potter needs a positive attitude, zeal, and self-discipline before he can successfully produce wares. In other cultures, a beginning potter may think nothing of spending five or more years, full time, as an apprentice before his or her pieces are considered worth keeping. Our attitude is not that stringent because the cultural condition has changed and because there is much that can be learned from pieces that are flawed—if only to establish a benchmark for developing discrimination as to what makes a pot of lasting interest.

Minimal Requirements of Productivity:
1) Ten completed bowls
2) Ten completed forms that are more closed than open (bottles, spheres, jars, etc.)
3) Two completed pinched, coiled, or slab pieces (i.e., hand built)

Among these twenty-two should be, at least:
1) One sgraffito piece (design scratched through a colored slip to reveal the base clay underneath)
2) One slip-painted piece (base clay coated completely or partially with liquid clay of a contrasting color)
3) One wax resist slip-decorated piece (base clay stopped out by wax resist and covered with a contrasting slip that will adhere only where there is no wax)
4) One two-piece form (for example, a lidded piece or a piece with handles)
5) One piece in which the exterior is unglazed and stained with iron oxide (most suitable to a textured clay or surface)

These requirements insure an elementary grasp of the range and potential of the potter's art. While quantity is no assurance of quality, it is unlikely that beginners will arrive at quality pieces without some quantitative base and a range of variety. There will be ample opportunity for individual expression within and beyond these requirements.

The nature of the course is such that *attendance and practice are mandatory.* Students must practice on their own as well as in class. Regular attendance is necessary because there are habits and methods that transcend the individual learner (but not his or her individuality), and it is important that these be established from the start.

Each student must keep a "claying journal" in which a dialogue with the clay and a dialogue with the self about the clay are set down at least once a week (preferably after each day's efforts). Journals will be collected at the fifth and ninth weeks, and we will discuss your progress. The writing may be subjective, reflective, descriptive.

The skills and attitudes germane to this course have something in common with dance, sports, yoga, aikido, tai chi, and the like, in which body-mind integration and awareness through movement and full participation are essential. The attitude is wholistic: the organic use of all of one's faculties in an alert but relaxed and concentrated manner. Recommended readings along this line are *Zen in the Art of Archery,* by Eugene Herrigel; *The Inner Game of Tennis,* by Timothy W. Galwey; and *Golf in the Kingdom,* by Michael Murphy.

Imagery and imitation are important methods of learning; therefore, one of my assistants—or I myself—will work a part of each four-hour session. While he or she is working, students may watch but are not to interrupt or talk to him or her. If there are questions, direct them to the teacher who is actively instructing at that time.

We will prepare many of our own clays, slips, and glazes, do our own clean-up and prepare for and care for our own firings, and *all students will be expected to enter into communal tasks.* Pottery is a very physical art, not one for spectators or dilettantes.

Development of skills will vary greatly among students. Try not to compare yourself with the person on the next wheel. Concentrate on yourself and the clay; a patient, focused, but relaxed attitude will usually pay off in greater degrees of awareness and control. Try to see how a total movement is performed without getting overly concerned about fine details. Mental rehearsal and practice are also recommended—the quiet visualization of successful actions. Zen potters meditate before beginning, to quiet the mind's incessant chatter. To this end, guided fantasy, autogenic visualization, self-instruction, and the courting of intuition are all worthy of exploration. The very way one breathes is related to how one performs. Try to leave your problems outside the pottery room and your work here can be satisfying, even therapeutic.

Grading will be based on quality of work, attitude, participation, zeal, integration, and progress from one's own benchmark.

Tentative Schedule: Some of the terms in the following descriptions will, of course, be unfamiliar. At the end of ten weeks, students will be comfortable with the terms and their applications.

Week 1: Introduction. Wedging clay by kneading. Moving the clay on the wheel. Centering.

Week 2: Refinements of techniques learned in Week 1. Opening up; drawing up the wall. Removing a piece from the mound. Introduction of the general ritual, as follows (throwing off the mound):

Before the wheel: Wedging 100 turns. Clay shaped into "watermelon" form.

On the wheel: Clay rhythmically clapped with dry hands into approximate center, then:

1. Cone raised and lowered three times (Cone 3 times)
2. Knob of desired quantity fixed on fourth time up (Fix knob)
3. Opening cone with thumbs and raising into cylinder (one movement). Additional drawing up, as needed. (Open and raise cylinder)
4. Choke
5. Thin
6. Finish edge
7. First tweak
8. *Oshibera,* for setting final shape
9. Second tweak
10. Cut with string
11. Remove with two hands at tweak. Take shapes as far through the process as possible. If a bowl emerges on the board, study it, cut it in half and examine the cross section.

Week 3: Repeat of weeks 1 and 2. If any forms come off the wheel well, consider saving them for tooling introduction (week 4 or end of week 3). Sometime during this week, we will learn how to make *oshibera* ribs and perhaps a bottling tool.

Week 4: Controlled tooling. Making *kannas* for tooling. Setting up a chuck for tooling.

Week 5: Repeats of preceding weeks, plus simple bottles from the mound. Hand in journals.

Week 6: Repeats of preceding weeks, plus tooling bottles. Use of slips, carving, and the like, before bisque firing. Use of bisque kilns.

Week 7: Introduction to raku clay. Bowls and small bottles in raku clay. Pinching (make sure you mark which of your pots are in raku clay for later firing). Preparation of high-fire glazes. Glazing.

Week 8: Repeats of preceding weeks, plus first stoneware firing. End of wet work.

Week 9: Finishings. Second stoneware firing. Journals are due.

Week 10: Third stoneware firing. Raku firing. Deep breathing.

Native Stoneware Clay

Of course, clay can be purchased from commercial suppliers, but it is highly preferable to dig the clay yourself, if possible. The best way to judge a new clay deposit is to ask yourself several questions about it, as you feel it and observe it closely: Is it hard to dig or prepare, with too many stones or impurities? Is it plastic enough or too plastic? Will it throw and dry and tool well? Will it withstand high temperatures? Will it take glazes well? and so forth. For years, I have gone to the same secret place in a wooded area near my home and brought back to my studio a native stoneware clay. I can sing the praises of this clay as highly as the native porcelain stone of Arita. It makes possible "Penn-*yaki*," or local Pennsylvania pottery, as one of my Japanese friends jokingly calls it.

This clay is heavy in iron, though its purer strains are almost completely a light gray, only here and there streaked with salmon. It must also be high in alumina, for it can withstand high stoneware temperatures and even go in and out of the shock of a raku firing. (Pots and other wares made by the raku technique are fired rapidly and cooled even more rapidly. Thus it is essential that the clay be porous enough to withstand the stress of these sudden thermal changes.) In its plasticity, the clay is like a pure ball clay (fine-grained, highly plastic), though it surpasses any ball clay I know in this regard. It is usually devoid of stones, although it may contain an occasional hemlock root or a bit of decomposed twig.

When I dig down a foot or so to get this clay, cutting through humus and sandy areas and roots, the hole usually begins to fill with water. So the clay, though very dense, comes out wet and plastic. I have often brought it back to my studio and used it directly, breaking it down by pinching it into small pieces or beating it out into thin sheets with a wooden club. These processes reveal impurities and non-plastic areas in the clay, also breaking it down so that it can be combined with a small amount of water and worked up for use (also known as wedging, which will be discussed later in this chapter).

My students and I will sometimes trample the clay with bare feet in a large mortar-mixing trough, adding water and other materials (sand and fireclay) as needed. The clay trampler goes round and round, wedging the clay thus with overlapping foot strokes. It is a beautiful process, though quite laborious.

I have also prepared clay using settling pools. Three such pools are usually used. Dried and pulverized clay is stirred into a slurry in one pool or container and allowed to settle briefly. Then it is decanted or dripped off only the top portion of this pool or container, into a second pool. The same process is repeated from the second to the third pool. The third pool has the finest grains, the first the coarsest. Clay thus prepared is liquid and must be dried out slowly for use and therefore takes longer to prepare. The clear water on the tops of containers is siphoned off before pouring the slurry into drying vats or onto drying bats.

This clay throws extremely well; true, like ball clay, it will undergo more than average shrinkage, and it will sometimes crack, especially on the bottom. But when submitted to a stoneware wood-firing in a Japanese hill kiln (*noborigama*), where the fire moves up the hill from one continuous chamber to another, the clay undergoes subtle quiet color changes, similar to those in Japanese Bizen wares—from grays to oranges, browns, purplish blues, and brown greens; and if the potter combines patience and spirit in the proper stoking of the kiln, parts of the clay emerge with glazed areas from the fly ash of the wood fire.

For other uses, I add to this clay sand and fireclay (a rough-textured, dark clay that is not very plastic and withstands high temperatures), to open it up, give it texture, and improve its drying and tooling characteristics. I also make a beautiful orange raku clay from it by adding equal parts of yellow sand and fireclay. This same mix is excellent for large stonewares. Its color has earned it the name "potter's gold." I will often wedge some of this clay into other clays that I have prepared, using sources from commercial clay mines. Its color, plasticity, and texture set it apart from the standard mined clays I know.

The impact such a clay has on students and fellow potters has almost always been positive and inspirational. Former students will return from many miles away to get several balls of it, which they will horde or treasure for special work. Those who know this clay can always spot it in a fired piece. The clay's surface, when tooled or left as thrown, will later show pits and markings where organic matter has burnt away, or where iron has melted down. And its iron content is such that it will stain slips and glazes used over it. Salt glazing and Shino-type glazes do not take to the straight native clay well. But in other cases, from wood-firing to carving through white or black slip under ash glaze, a subtle and natural fire-pot-glaze transformation and unity result.

Wedging

The start of the throwing process involves preparing clay for the wheel, or *wedging*—kneading the clay into a homogeneous mass that is free of air bubbles and lumps. A well-wedged mound of clay is the first pre-requisite for throwing a pot. In Japan, wedging is referred to as *chrysan-themum* or *spiral* kneading, because the pressures of the rhythmic rocking and twisting motions leave a beautifully ordered series of indentations and overlaps on the clay, reminiscent of the petals of a chrysanthemum (Plate 5).

As is the case with all of the steps in the traditional lessons I am pre-senting, wedging is never completely mastered. It remains a barometer of the potter's body-mind as he or she makes ready for the wheel. It gives immediate feedback on whether the mind is elsewhere, or ahead of itself. Wedging can be a strenuous process, but it should not be overly so, for one's energies must be contained and conserved, and yet totally applied. In a sense, wedging is the potter's aerobic training, for turning a sizable lump of clay one, two, or three hundred times is indeed a workout.

Experienced potters get to know their clay in wedging. As they pre-pare the clay for the wheel, they also prepare themselves for it. While wedging, the potter finds out whether the clay is too soft or too hard, too "short" or too "long" (terms used to express the clay's cohesive plasticity), too grainy or too smooth. As for the number of turns required before the clay is the proper working consistency, I usually wedge stoneware two hundred turns, and porcelain three hundred, reversing the clay and resting after each hundred.

To understand how to position the hands during wedging, the beginner must realize that the finished product will be cone-shaped. The left hand, which lifts and twists the cone, also collects the clay at the broad end of the cone, so it is always placed over the bottom of the cone. The right hand is placed on the side of the cone, at the bottom edge. It is the right hand's pressure, along with the rocking motion, that creates the new "petal" in each turn.

To start, the clay is pushed into a rough cone shape. The left hand, cupped over the bottom of the cone, lifts it up on its point with a spiral motion, and the right hand presses down on the clay, folding inward some clay from behind. Again, the left hand lifts up the cone, the right hand presses down again, folding more clay from behind, and so on. It is important to remember that the clay is rotated only while the left hand is lifting it, and is pressed down straight, without rotation, by the right hand.

When the last turn is made, the wedging continues, but, in order to collect the clay together now in a shape ready for the wheel, with each turn the right hand drops down slightly toward the wedger. This stops new petals from forming and collects the open end of the spiraling conical shell back into the mass. Finally, the potter brings his two feet together by moving forward with the left, then completes the work with a rocking, slapping motion of the two hands. The end product is a bullet-like shape, flattened on the bottom (as it stands on its end), tall and slightly conical and rounded on the top.

Beginners are often puzzled by wedging, so I recommend that they watch, then work beside an experienced wedger. Often I have them start with "ram's head" bread-kneading motions—so called because the clay takes on the shape of a ram's head and horns. By turning the flattened-out ram's head around and starting from a new angle, one slowly slips into a rhythm, thereby avoiding the flattening out that grounds the rhythmic continuity of this approach. To keep a ram's head rolling, one must pick up and put more pressure on one hand, thus rendering the shape of the clay asymmetrical. After watching and then imitating an experienced wedger, the beginner is ready to try the real thing. The ideal is to contain rocking, rolling, and wrapping the clay up inside itself in a rhythmic manner, so that the clay basically stays in one place, and doesn't "walk away" from the wedger (as it invariably does with a beginner).

The wedging surface must be so sturdy that it won't move at all while the potter is at work. Its height varies with that of the potter, but 26 to 28 inches (66 to 71 cm.) is a good average height. A wood surface with a hard, but non-splintering textured grain is best. Some wood can be singed with a blowtorch and then scrubbed with a wire brush to hasten the natural aging process, which leaves the hard grain raised over the soft. The clay will not stick to such a surface.

The potter's stance while wedging is important: the feet should be about 2 feet (61 cm.) apart, right foot slightly forward. When an experienced potter wedges clay, his whole body is involved. The power of his stomach, back, and shoulders is especially evident, as bodily energy seems to flow off the shoulders into the wedging. Here, again, the stance echoes that of aikido, where the *hara*—the body's center of gravity— keeps the body grounded and lets force flow from that center. From this position, the body easily rocks to and fro with each turn of the clay, but it cannot be pushed off-center by the clay. When a larger ball of clay is being wedged, the body rocks more vigorously and may rise slightly on the toes, but it is still grounded, in control of the clay.

When wedging goes well, it seems as though the clay is wedging itself. For beginners, imagery, reinforcement, correction, and repetition are the best method I know of learning to wedge. Over the years, I have learned to slow down the process sufficiently so I can verbalize it while students watch; pointing out the steps at slow speed helps correct some beginners, but the analytical breakdown in words hopelessly entangles others. This is a problem that will recur in other aspects of our lessons: the verbal analytic explanation that helps intellectual understanding but often impedes wholistic action. Applied when the problem or error in action is nearing the threshold of awareness, however, the verbal analytical explanation can lead to insight and integration.

Centering

Beginners are often taught to form pots from small balls of clay sufficient for only one finished piece. In Japan, however, apprentices take to the wheel as much clay as they can comfortably wedge at one time— usually enough for ten or more small bowls or bottles. Throwing several shapes off one large mound of clay is called "throwing on the hump," or "throwing on the mound." The advantage of this method is that the entire body-mind must come to grips with the reality of wheel–clay–potter as one moving but centered whole.

A vital part of the throwing process, centering involves moving the thoroughly wedged, bullet-shaped mound of clay into a perfectly symmetrical position on the wheelhead. The clay is gently set on the wheelhead, as close to the center as possible, and then, without kicking the wheel, the potter rhythmically claps the palms of both hands, fingers relaxed, on the surface of the mound, so that the wheel moves slowly in the kicking direction. The clapping motion moves from the bottom to the top of the mound; even at this point, the potter is feeling for roundness and center.

Slip (clay the consistency of mayonnaise) and water are spread over the entire surface of the mound as the wheel is kicked into counterclockwise motion (in Japan, the wheel is kicked in a clockwise direction). Both hands are placed on the clay, starting at the top of the mound and moving as far down toward the wheel head as feels comfortable, to smooth out the mound and get it into a more uniform shape. With large mounds of clay, it usually takes repeated downward movements to smooth out wrinkles and establish a point of center at the top.

At this point, the first of three raisings and lowerings into a tall cone begins. The hands are placed opposite one another on the clay, near the bottom of the cone. Pressure is applied, so that a ball-like indentation is formed near the bottom of the mound (very important for beginners). The hands slowly but steadily move up toward the top edge of the mound, so that a tall narrow cone shape is achieved. The back and inside surface edge of the palms are the pressure points that move and lift the mound. If the hands move too fast from bottom to top, a spiral will be created; too little pressure with the hands, and the cone will not be formed; too much pressure, and the clay will be tweaked off at the top.

The first time up is the most difficult, for the mound of clay has memories of wedging, clapping, and off-centeredness within it. Beginners will repeatedly lose the ball or move too fast or too slowly, out of harmony with wheel speed and clay movement. Tweaking off the top of the mound is a better sign than not moving it at all, for at least this shows the application of energy. If only the surface of the clay is pulled up, with not enough pressure exerted toward the center of the cone, the top of the mound will show a hollow. Pressure must press inward as well as upward to thin out the top of the mound into a tall cone.

When first learning to kick the flywheel, beginners often move their bodies, and thus their hands. The hands should resist the clay, not move with it, and the beginner should make a concerted effort to bring kicking, hands, and entire body into harmony with the wheel and the clay from the start. Motorized wheels are not the blessing an undisciplined and technological culture presumes them to be, for the wheel runs away with potter and clay, literally keeping one out of touch with the core and surface of the mound of clay.

When raising the cone, I tend to exert pressure on the mound somewhat asymmetrically. (My teacher's motions with his hands appeared to be symmetrical, as though he were raising a window from a crouched position with hands and forearms.) But I find I drive the clay with less effort by pushing from slightly under the left hand with my right hand. When I use a motor wheel, the lift is felt through the whole body, up from the balls of the feet. On a kick wheel, the potter uses the foot rests as the springing ground when not kicking, and maintains a subtle balance between one foot rest and the moving foot when kicking the flywheel.

Let us assume the mound has been raised into a tapering cone twice its original height. Now it must be lowered back into a smoother and more compact mound. This is done by leaning the clay visibly into the wheel direction. For counter-clockwise spin, the thumb of the left hand rests lightly on the center on the top of the cone while the ball of the palm under the thumb tilts the cone toward a two o'clock position on the wheel head (the potter sits at six o'clock). The left hand pushes the clay down, and because of this movement, the tilt of the left hand, and the torque of the wheel, the cone is collapsed back inside itself.

As with raising the mound into a cone, so lowering it by tilting into the wheel motion requires a feel for the still core of the clay. I tell beginners to imagine a steel rod in the center of the clay against which they can lean. This imaginary rod is equilibrium, where the give-and-take between body and clay balance out, both in motion and dynamic, both at rest. In tilting the cone to lower it, the wheel torque will force the hand back and in the wheel direction.

The whole body needs to absorb this force slowly, and again, in equilibrium. The force against the cone is repaid by an equal force back. By returning with that force to center and changing hand positions— the right hand moves to the top of the mound as the left hand crosses toward the front of the potter and drops to the bottom of the mound—the mound settles down into a compact mass and on center.

This was the first raising and lowering. Though several steps are necessary, when properly done, it is one effortless and graceful motion. This process is repeated a second and third time. By now, clay, potter, and wheel are one and ready to proceed.

During the raising and lowering process, it is important to keep the clay from drying out, making the proper management of slip and water essential. Slip should be carefully wrung from the hands before it is applied to the clay. I usually wring my left hand with my right, then my right with my left, and deposit the accumulated slip in my right hand. From there I reapply it to the surface of the mound. I let a few drops of water run down my fingertips onto the slipped surface, and then move my fingers gently up and down to mix the slip and water. When there is more slip than needed, it is returned to a special part of the water pan; in Japan, it is deposited on the pan's right front edge. In time, the fingers become skilled at separating out any lumps of clay that find their way into the slip. Lumps are dropped into the water toward the left of the water pan. Insignificant as this procedure may seem, beginners must learn it, for slip, lumps, and water are typically mixed in confusion, and this can be detrimental to the processes described here. Tradition and trust establish the right practice for the good of learning.

Forming on the Mound

I will start a discussion of forming with the universal bowl shape. Later, I will expand it to a simple bottle shape—more closed than open—and to a simple plate, all from the mound.

The bowl is best indicated by a cupping together of the two hands. It is not a flat container with straight sides. This flowing, unending form is at the same time simple, complex, and beautiful. I never tire of it, nor of its infinite variations of fullness, ripeness, shallowness, deepness, generosity, guardedness. But this form must be learned correctly in throwing. If the center is raised or too low, the flow is broken. If the wall was mistreated in earlier stages, the "memory" within the clay's history will show up as a break in the bowl's generous opening continuity. As with a parabola, the curve of a bowl is infinite, embracing the universe.

The fourth raising of the cone is part of forming. The ball that is being passed up the cone stops short of the top. The right hand retains its cupped hollow and relaxes as the left hand moves to the top of the cone and presses gently down. The top pressure is released and the right hand is left spinning briefly before it is also withdrawn.

The shape that results from this is a ball on a tapering stem; the stem-like shape is quite important to later operations. The ball, referred to in Japan as the *fixed quantity*, is relative to the size of bowl being made.

Slip and a few drops of water are spread over the ball in preparation for opening it. Opening may be done in one flowing motion or in stages. (I prefer one flowing motion, but the right thumb can make the first penetration, moving quickly down beyond the knuckle from a cupped hand position and leaning slightly out to open the top of the stem more than the bottom.) To open up the ball in one motion, the hands are cupped around the ball, fingertips touching in front and remaining so throughout the procedure. Both thumbs plunge in steadily and directly to the bottom, whence they start to press toward the palm of the hand, forcing the walls of the opening upward. By keeping the fingertips together at all times, the opening and rising cylinder is kept from spreading out too fast into a wide bowl or dish shape. Slightly tilting back the hands at the wrists, engaging the lower fingertips more, aids in choking the cylinder in as it is being pinched up by the thumbs.

With this one motion, properly executed, the potter has the beginning cylinder for a bowl, sweeping in one continuous shape from the central low point to the tapered top edge. After this comes a choking upward, starting on the stem beneath the opened ball. This assures the flow from stem to bowl and keeps the walls tightened in for the next operation.

For shaping and thinning, the right hand should be relaxed, falling into a natural cupped and rounded form, which will provide the hollow armature for the first shaping of the bowl. The fingertips of the right hand should lightly encircle the stem, to insure that the bowl buds out from the stem itself. The left hand then finds the inside center, presses down slightly (each new forming requires some pressing down to retain a roundness from true center), and sweeps out against the bowl-like shape of the restraining right hand. When the fingers of the left hand have moved into the palm area of the right hand, the right hand begins moving upward, the left hand slows down, and the fingertips of both hands reach the top edge together. This is an ideal form for beginners, because as a rule, they will need to make several attempts at each of the steps involved before the flowing bowl shape emerges.

The bowl may be thinned or refined further by fingertips, or the final shape may be set using a pushing rib, or *oshibera*. This rib is in the shape of a cross-section of the desired bowl, from center through the curve and extending to the top rim or beyond. It is cut from a thin, grainy wood (various pines and cedars are used in Japan) about 3/8 inch (10 mm.) thick, in such a way that the curve is penetrated at its fastest turn by the grain of the wood. This gives a tooth to the edge, which prevents the rib from sticking to the clay. (The close-grained hard wooden tools with smoother edges sold at pottery supply houses are worst for this purpose.) Since this rib will be used in the dominant or right hand, it is shaped with the curve facing to the left. A bevel of about 3/8 inch (10 mm.) is cut along the edge to collect any slip remaining, and to pack the edge with the sharpened edge only. The wheel will spin clockwise for this operation, since the right hand will now be inside the bowl.

Before using the oshibera, the bowl's rim should be smoothed with a piece of chamois held between the thumb and forefingers of both hands, by gently applying it to the rim while the bowl is revolving. (I usually start the wheel going clockwise at this point.) After this, the first tweak is made on the stem beneath the bowl, at least 1/2 inch (13 mm.) down from the bowl hollow, or else there will be no foot and the bowl will be misshaped by both tweaking it and lifting it from the mound later. (A tweak may be defined as an abrupt narrowing of the stem of the mound of clay, like a marked groove or indentation. It sets off the work nearing completion from the remaining mound of clay and serves, in addition, clear functions in the completion and removal of the piece, as outlined below.) The tweak is made using the two first fingers of the left hand, palm up, in a scissors-like motion, slightly pulling back and downward as the fingers are closed gently together. With practice, the feel of center is grasped in tweaking so that the bowl's position on the stem is left unchanged.

The tweak indentation now becomes the guiding groove for the fingertips of the left hand. The thumb of the left hand is placed on the upper point of the oshibera, now firmly held by fingers and thumb of the right hand. The wheel is set in motion by the left foot, and with the outer curve of the oshibera, the potter moves the side of the bowl outward until the point is at true center, at which time the oshibera, held at about nine o'clock on the wheel and in a straight line but top tilted toward the potter so he can see over it, is pressed firmly down, turned slowly toward the potter (toward six o'clock) as it is raised and finishes the curve of the sides.

Again, this operation requires constant practice. The oshibera will imprint a flawless curve on the bowl if the steps previous to its use have been well executed. If the wall of the bowl is too thin, too thick, or irregular, or if the bottom does not flow continuously into the sides, this will show up in the final form. The oshibera will not correct a bad history in the piece; on the contrary, the oshibera will accentuate such flaws.

Also, if the rib is not held at the right angle so that the center is only gently lower than the rest, a funnel shape will result. This suggests, as well, that the rib be shaped in such a way that it is almost, but not quite, flat as it approaches center. As with all these processes, imagery, purpose, and practice shape as much as do tools and methods.

Now, after this third forming step, whether by fingers (as in the Japanese ceremonial tea bowl) or by the oshibera, the bowl is ready to be removed from the mound or hump. A final tweak is made, thinning further the attachment to the stem. The bowl is cut free in the middle of the tweak, which is made below the foot. (Later I will describe, when I discuss porcelain, how string is used to cut while in motion.) Forming a V between the two middle fingers on each hand, palms up, the potter picks up the bowl at the tweak. By using the two middle fingers instead of the first and second (which usually seems more natural to a beginner), the thumbs are kept well away from the sides of the bowl. This is especially advantageous when removing larger bowls or plates from the mound.

These, then, are the steps in making a bowl: forming the ball, opening and drawing up the cylinder, shaping the bowl, finishing the edge, first tweak, refining the form (by fingers or oshibera), second tweak, cutting, and removing. They constitute a kind of catechism of traditional practice on this beginning, universal bowl form. They also set habits and sensitivities for most of what will follow in other forms and processes. As in all traditional arts involving holistic participation of the body-mind, they are never completely mastered. They introduce the beginner, however, to the authentic world of forming within the Great Tradition. We will see how other steps tie directly into the spirit and economy of these.

Tooling

There are short-cuts in any discipline, but they are bought at the cost of true freedom and spontaneity. For a beginner, tooling in the Japanese tradition is at first as hard as throwing, moving clay on the wheel, and wedging. The form that was lovingly shaped through the preceding steps will flow into its naked and revealed form naturally through tooling. This is the ideal. Love for tools, for the grace and economy of actions, for the profile to be liberated, and for the live balance of the basic footed bowl in one's hands absorbs tooling into the spirit of making pottery.

For the bowl that does not reverse its wall direction by a counter-curve at its rim, one simple metal cutting tool—or *kanna*, as it is called in Japanese—will suffice. The metal band used around lumber and large packages, 1/2 to 1 inch (13 to 26 mm.) in width, makes a good kanna. Cut a piece with clean straight right angles 7 to 9 inches (18 to 23 cm.) long. Using a vice with metal jaws and a ball peen hammer or equivalent, bend one end to a sharp or clean-cornered right angle one inch (26 mm.) from the end. Make sure the corner is not rounded or vague. Bend the other end in the other direction in a right angle about 1/2 inch (13 mm.) from the end.

Hold the kanna, with the left hand, on the edge of a wooden table or counter, corner at the left, shaft perpendicular to the filer. Using a straight-sided metal file about eight inches (20 cm.) long, begin filing

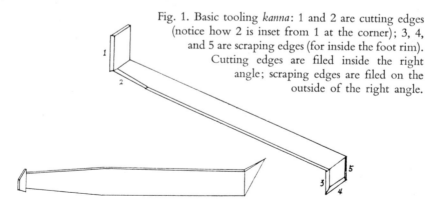

Fig. 1. Basic tooling *kanna*: 1 and 2 are cutting edges (notice how 2 is inset from 1 at the corner); 3, 4, and 5 are scraping edges (for inside the foot rim). Cutting edges are filed inside the right angle; scraping edges are filed on the outside of the right angle.

Fig. 2. Carving *kanna*: The keystone-like form and pointed end are used for all types of carving (see page 97).

the 1-inch (26 mm.) end with smooth strokes from the inside corner to the outer edge. Each stroke down should evenly cover the entire surface, at about a 45-degree angle. File straight with the shaft of the kanna. Continue filing until the 45-degree edge breaks through to the other side. You can tell when this point has been reached, for a burr will be raised on the outside edge. Turn the kanna so that the shaft is parallel to you and file the other surface of the kanna intersecting with the edge just sharpened. Here, too, only about an inch (26 mm.) of the kanna is sharpened (more would make a knife-edge that would cut into the holding hand while tooling). This edge is filed until the intersecting corner drops about 1/16 inch (1.5 mm.) lower than the first edge. It is important not to turn the file, in order to retain the pointed corner and dropped edge. (Fig. 1 shows the ideal relationship of these two cutting surfaces.) These two shaped edges, coming together at different levels, constitute a dynamic cutting point, while the 1-inch (26 mm.) flat blade becomes a precise shaving and smoothing edge that will not catch at the corner because the meeting edge is lowered. Several counterstrokes with the file from the opposite side of the sharpened edges removes the burr, leaving clean, razor-sharp edges.

The opposite, shorter right-angled end of the kanna is filed on the outside. This end is used for scraping and is especially useful for finishing the inside foot-rim at the end of the tooling process. Here all three edges of the bent end are filed at a 45-degree angle. The right-handed outer corner of this end, when the bend is facing downward, can be slightly rounded, for it will scrape the inside corner of the foot ring and rounding will soften the severity of the join with the bowl bottom. In a later refinement, potters sometimes make this corner somewhat longer than the inner or left-handed corner of the kanna, since the bowl curves slightly toward the foot ring. But at the beginning, a straight cut is simpler.

As with all instruments where an art is involved, it pays to have a number of such kanna available. One will often feel or work better on a particular piece. Some cutting edges can be longer or shorter than 1 inch (26 mm.), thus extending the variety of alternatives. The scraping end can also be made deeper and longer to accommodate a range of foot rims. (Later I will describe a curved equivalent of this kanna, used for concave rather than convex surfaces.)

A second aspect of tooling precision lies in the use of the tooling chuck (Plate 6). A chuck is a thrown, hollow conical armature, open at top and bottom, on which a clay cushion or ring is placed to hold the pot to be tooled. Bowls and plates are tooled on the outside of a chuck head; spheres and bottles on the inside or within the chuck ring. Beginners often make the mistake of not using a chuck, and simply fasten the bowl rim down with clay directly on the wheel head. The disadvantages of this method are legion. The edge is often strained or ruined, the form and weight cannot be easily checked, and the entire outer surface cannot be tooled or thinned, if desired. A bowl must be free to be seen, handled, and weighed. It must, in short, be loose but free and centered, just as in throwing. This requires a dynamic, not static, collaboration of the potter's body-mind with the bowl and the tooling process.

Chucks can be kept active for a year or more by keeping them properly dampened and wrapped in plastic. While the chuck is being used, bands of cloth dipped in slip can be wrapped on the edge of the chuck where clay and the bisque meet. This method further prevents bisque and clay from separating.

For small bowls the size beginners will make, 4 to 6 inches (10 to 15 cm.) in diameter, a bisque chuck should be 6 to 9 inches (15 to 23 cm.) high, the bottom about 5 inches (13 cm.) in diameter and tapering to a 2-inch (5 cm.) top diameter. This bisque form should be soaked in water until it is thoroughly dampened, then set down on the wheel head to be centered.

With the wheel set in motion, the potter taps the chuck with the outer edge of the right hand, palm opened, at about three o'clock on the wheel head. A syncopated rhythm is required, for hand and eye are not initially coordinated in this action. Sighting along the right side of the rotating chuck, the potter taps his right hand after the chuck's off-center edge goes by three o'clock. If the tap is made at the very moment the off-center bump is at three o'clock, the chuck will only become more off-center. It takes quite a bit of practice, in a relaxed but sensitive attitude, to learn the rhythm necessary for this procedure. Once centered, the chuck is held firmly with the left hand as the right hand attaches pieces of plastic clay coils (first dipped in water) where chuck and wheel-head meet. If the clay coils are not wetted, they will not adhere to the bisque; and if the bisque chuck has not been dampened, it will dry the coil prematurely and cause it to crack or come loose.

At the top, tooling end of the chuck, a ball of clay with a tail formed to fit inside the chuck head is pushed down on the wet chuck rim. Both clay and chuck head can be moistened just as the two are pressed together, keeping water off the top of the ball. Then, the clay at the join is pressed around the chuck neck. Next, using extended fingers or a canvas-covered paddle, the chuck head is paddled to a flat and straight-sided form. Using a needle first, then a kanna, the chuck head is then tooled to a flat-topped, straight-sided cylindrical top, the diameter of which is such that it engages the curve of the bowl about halfway up its sides. If the bowl sits too low in the chuck, there won't be enough support; too high, and the rim will be unduly strained. Precision of centering and a straight edge are essential, for a bowl cannot be centered on an off-center chuck.

Beginners tend to think that a chuck with a rounded shape will hold a bowl—or any other rounded form—best. But that isn't so; a straight edge, at right angles, tapered only 1/8 inch (3 mm.) on a 45-degree angle, is ideal for these shapes.

The chuck is allowed to dry until it is firm—this can take several hours. Drying can be expedited by sprinkling dried clay shavings or chips about 1/2 inch (13 mm.) deep on the moist top surface. The dry chips will soak up the clay's excess moisture. As soon as the chuck is firm, the bowl—neither too damp nor too dry, but leather hard—is placed rim down on the chuck head, and is tapped gently on center with the fingers of the right hand. The first or second finger of the left hand spins on the base of the upside-down bowl to contain the tap of the right hand and keep the bowl from going off-center. Once the bowl has found its best center, a V cut is made firmly on center of the unfinished foot base with the right angle of the cutting-end of the kanna. Here, too, practice is necessary, for this V cut is the home center where the loose bowl is held in place by the first or second finger of the left hand while the tooling is being done with the right hand. It took me quite a while to master this. One thing is certain: Unless the bowl, the V cut, and the chuck are on center, precise tooling is impossible.

The first tooling cut is made at the intersection of bowl and stem. A right-angled cut at this point can next be integrated downward into the rounded bowl, and upward into the straight side of the foot. The top edge is trued. All of this is done with the point of the right angle, where the two blades of the kanna come together. Then the flat blade of the cutting end makes a pass from foot-bowl corner to the edge of the rim. All the while, the first or second finger of the left hand exerts sufficient downward pressure to hold the bowl in place. The thumb of the left hand rides on the upper outside corner of the kanna (the non-cutting surface), thus linking left and right hands together as one unit, and con-

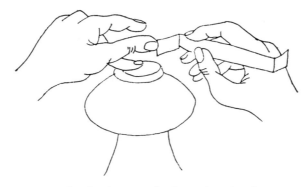

Fig. 3. How hands relate to each other and to a bowl on a chuck in tooling with the basic *kanna*.

trolling the amount of pressure to be placed on the cutting blades. The right hand holds the kanna with thumb inside, forefinger on top, second finger underneath, choking up on the angle (see Fig. 3).

This procedure is continued until the proper foot width and bowl thickness and balance are achieved. It is important to feel the wall repeatedly, with thumb and forefinger, testing for uniform thickness. I often find that when I tool a series of bowls, I must come back and redo my first ones, for by that time they feel too heavy in comparison with the last tooled ones.

At this point, the inside of the foot is hollowed out. Using the corner of the kanna, pressure is applied straight down into the V-shaped finger hole. This method can clean out most of the clay inside the emerging foot. It takes courage and practice to develop the feel for it, for the down pressure of the kanna is all that holds the bowl in place. Then the scraping end of the kanna (the smaller end with outside filing) is used, moving from center to edge of the hollowed-out foot, with right thumb on top of the kanna, and right forefinger on the outside of the foot. This motion is repeated until the desired thickness of the emerging foot band and of the base of the bowl is achieved. Tapping with the forefinger gives auditory feedback on the thickness of the base of the bowl. If the sound is hollow, it is thin enough.

When I began as a potter, I was enamored of my own thumb prints and throwing marks, and would not tool much. I have long since abandoned this often misplaced spontaneity in favor of the freer spontaneity of form and balance for eye and hand. Yet, as in the ceremonial Japanese tea bowl, I can honor the subtle asymmetry of finger pressure and not tool a finely potted bowl, except on the foot. Or, following Hamada and the mingei schools, I can let the edge of tooling stop sharply within the thrown area, especially where the change between thrown and tooled texture is part of the aesthetic surface of the piece. The beauty of these tooling methods is that once they are mastered, they can be used as much or as little on an individual piece as the potter desires.

Other Beginning Forms

When making bottles, spheres, or other closed forms, the same basic procedures as for forming bowls are followed, with the exception that the cylinder is one and one-half to two times as high as it is wide. This requires a larger and usually wider knob or ball at the top of the stem. Also, greater care in managing clay is necessary. In opening, the finger-tips of both hands must stay in touch and the pulling back or choking action must be intensified to keep the cylinder from spreading out. Proper control of slip is also essential: The thumbs can easily dry out if the passage up the cylinder is not continuous and smooth, and this can draw the cylinder off center, or cause the top half of the cylinder to twist the bottom half because of greater weight and increased friction. In opening the bottom of the bottle shape, the thumbs should also sweep out laterally to widen it differently from the bowl—the goal is a flat, widened bottom, not a heavy, overly narrow base.

This opening motion may well take two or three passes at first, but one continuous draw is the goal. As with the bowl on the mound, the cylinder is now choked in and up. The top is kept turned slightly inward and not allowed to get overly thin. The shoulder area must also be allowed some thickening strength, as must the belly, since the latter must expand the most and the shoulder must support itself and the top. If the bottom wall is still overly thick and the inner base overly narrow, a correcting movement can widen the bottom and draw the wall thickness upward.

Now the cylinder is ready for shaping. In this operation, fingertip to fingertip pressure is most sensitive; pressure now is not from both sides on the wall to thin it, but is rather passed out by the left hand from inside for the bottom half, and back in from the outside (with the right hand) for the top half. Beginners should aim for a simple barrel or parenthetical shape, with the curve at its widest at the midpoint of the cylinder.

Extra slip is placed on the top third of the shape at this point and an encircling, choking pressure brings the top lip or neck to a smaller diameter. (I use crossed thumbs and second fingers for this.) After each choking the wall of the choked part must be gently thrown (without excess thinning) and smoothed or the top will wrinkle and twist. The rule is: choke, throw, choke, throw. As the neck of the bottle is being narrowed, the wall gets thicker, so it's necessary to pull the wall of the neck gently, with fingertips, to thin and raise it.

I teach beginners the use of a bottling tool from the start. Fig. 4 shows the forms of these *hera,* or ribs. The bottling tool is made so that it can hook through a small opening at the top and push the entire bottle shape out without widening the top much, if at all. Again, I'll assume right-handed use of the tool, so the wheel must now go clockwise (kicked with the left foot) to accommodate the tool inside the form.

Working with the bottling tool is awkward at first, because wood is now where fingertips and nerve endings would like to be. With much practice, however, the "nerves" are felt at the end of the bottling tool, as vibrations, subtle though they are, are read through the pressure and feel of the tool transmitted to the right hand. The left hand feels the

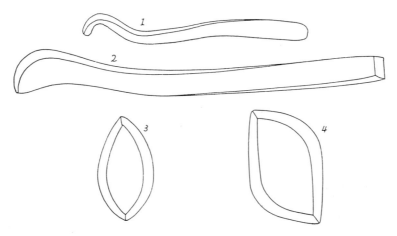

Fig. 4. Basic ribs used in throwing: 1 and 2, bottling tools; 3, all-purpose *oshibera;* 4, basic bowl *oshibera.*

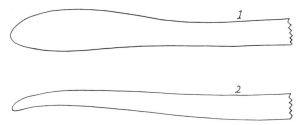

Fig. 5. Wooden wet-tooling blade: 1, top view; 2, side view. The tool is about 12 inches (30.5 cm.) long.

thrusting of the curve, now supports, now corrects, now leads, now follows the outward press. Repeated and daring expansions of the clay become progressively possible, so that a sphere can eventually become wider than high. To begin with, however, it is best to aim for a bottle shape with tightened top, not the widest curve, and some neck. These features are structurally stronger than those of a full sphere.

The bottle and sphere forms never seem to repeat themselves, so much does a slight variation in pressure change the character of the whole. As with the basic bowl, many, many spherical forms must be made for the body-mind and the clay forming to become one.

My students learn direct wet tooling as a first revelation of form of these shapes. For this, a curving wooden blade that also bends at the tip of its shaft is recommended (see Fig. 5). This tool is about 12 inches long, so that it can be grasped sturdily by both hands. The potter dismounts from the kick wheel to brace himself and to see the profile of the bottle while tooling. I usually drop down on one knee or sit on a stool beside the wheel. Pressure is slightly in as well as down for a smooth cut (if the cut is ragged, one is pulling out too much; if it goes into a spiral or jumps track, one has moved too fast or too erratically). The cut is begun where the wall of the outside starts its extra thickening from the stem of the mound to support the piece, or where the curve loses the clarity of its slope. A good cut makes the shape stand clean. Care must be taken to cut at least half an inch below the bottom hollow of the bottle. Then a needle is angled upward to remove this cut clay, meeting the bottle at the bottom of the cut. This is where the string is drawn through, also, in preparation for the form's removal from the wheel head. The bottle is picked up gently with both hands cupped evenly and lightly around the undercurve.

Tooling a bottle usually requires a kanna filed the same as the one for a bowl, but with the cutting end shaped like a half-moon arc and the scraping end like a semicircle. The filing of the edge is similar, except that one stroke will not go around the entire curve. The chuck head for a bottle is an open circle, so that the neck can fit down far enough so the bottom and foot can be tooled, and the bottom can fit so the top can be tooled. A doughnut of clay is pinched out, the surfaces of the bisque chuck and doughnut are wetted, and the doughnut is fused onto the centered bisque chuck. The shape of this chuck is a parabolic cylinder hollow at both ends, about 5 inches (13 cm.) wide, top and bottom, for beginning-size bottles (see Plate 6). Once it's been placed on the chuck, the top of the doughnut is paddled rhythmically on the sides and top with the fingers of both hands, or with a cloth-covered paddle, and as with the chuck for the basic bowl shape, the chuck is made flat-topped and straighted-sided through the use of needle and kanna, and then allowed to become firm.

When the bottle has dried to be leather hard, it is centered, head down, on the chuck. A V-shaped finger hole is first cut, as in the bowl, once the piece is centered. The regular kanna is used for all but concave or reverse curves, in which case the kanna with the arc-shaped cutting end is used. Often under the lip of a piece, the rounded scraping end must be used by angling it for the desired fit.

Beginners should measure the depth of the inside hollow first to ascertain how much clay is at the base. There can be much more rounding in of the bottom than wet tooling permits. Some potters do not tool their bottles and spheres at all; a heavier product that meets the surface on which it rests more bluntly is the likely outcome, but when crafted in the right hands, this has its own aesthetic potential.

When tooling a sphere, it is difficult at times to tool a foot on its true axis. One way to make sure that the piece is on center is to center it first upright, then make a horizontal line on the piece with a needle. When the piece is placed upside down and this line is again horizontal, then the axis is truly on center.

A few words here about the foot and lip of a bottle (I will go into more detail in the next chapter). Some potters do not like the foot and the top lip of a piece to be of the same diameter, but I have seen forms where this works perfectly well. I like bottles and spheres that have a definite, swelling curve under the lip, producing a quiet shadow under the fullness of the curve. And I usually set a sturdy but not overly high

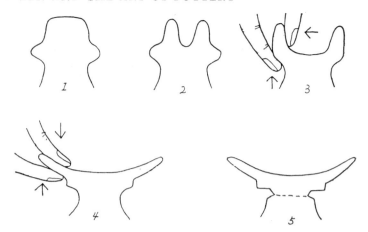

Fig. 6. Stages in throwing a plate from the mound: 1, the acorn-shaped ball; 2, opening the ball only as deep as the widest part of the acorn; 3, pushing the wall of the opening to the outer limit of the ball, supporting the acorn shape from below; 4, laying down the wall, with supporting pressure moving up to the plate's overhang; 5, the plate with concluding tweak, ready to cut with a string and pick up.

foot, angled at 45-degrees on the very bottom so that the curve of the belly is picked up by a receding foot edge.

The plate form thrown on the hump brings in several new features (see Fig. 6). The ball or fixed quantity is now wider and deeper. It is shaped somewhat like an acorn, with an expanded lower edge, 1/2 to 3/4 inch (13 to 19 mm.) thick. The upper portion of the ball is then opened straight up by the thumbs, not penetrating into the lower, wider portions. This opened wall is thinned slightly, then wheel direction is reversed, and the right hand placed inside. Supporting the base of the overhanging cylinder with left fingers, the right hand pushes the cylinder wall outward until the wall is now flush with the widest part of the ball (the earlier extended part of the acorn). The left hand then moves up to support the wall as it is moved or laid outward by the right hand and fingers. A tweak is then made under the base, and, while the fingers of the left hand support the bottom of the foot and the thumb rests on the top corner of an *oshibera* (or pushing rib), the flow of the plate is made continuous by the movement of the rib in the right hand, from center to rim. Sometimes a reverse or flattened rim of about 1/2 inch (13 mm.) is made to strengthen the plate.

Plates are tooled on a chuck, on the outside rim, as with the basic bowl. The bottle chuck's outside rim is an ideal first plate chuck. Tooling is the same as for the bowl, except for the accommodation necessary to the changed form.

When bowl, bottle, and plate forms are mastered so that the potter feels confidence and flow in their making, the foundation for larger or more complex forms has gracefully been laid. These are not "beginning" forms in the sense that they are left behind. They are never mastered completely, and one always needs to renew one's sensibilities and insights into their basic but infinite meaning.

Simple Additions to Basic Shapes

In beginning lessons I try to include a few pots made more complex by the addition of a lid, handle, or spout. But there are other organic routes to complexity, like the combination of wheel and hand work on one piece, or the addition of a coil to the top shoulder of a bottle that is thrown into a new neck and lip, or the tall stem of a goblet. All of these put a new demand on the unity of a form.

Simplicity is a virtue in such additions and extensions of a basic piece. In the case of lids, those that fit by means of friction or gravity, without complicated grooves and lips, are a good starting place. Fig. 7 shows a friction fit (curved surface on curved surface), a simple overlaid cap (as in a ginger jar), a cap with a lip and insert, and a gravity drop lid which hangs from a raised or flat lip (as in a teapot). All of these are easily en-

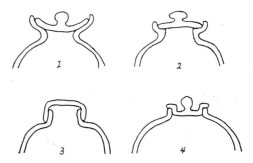

Fig. 7. Simple lids: 1, friction fit, curved surface on curved surface; 2, flat lid with insert lip; 3, cap or ginger jar lid; 4, hanging or drop lid.

gineered from the mound of clay and can be removed by means of a lifting tweak below the first string cut at the base of the lid proper. The two pieces of clay are separated after the lid has hardened sufficiently to be handled.

Although pulling handles from a fat coil insures a form aesthetically pleasing and in harmony with the thrown piece to which it will be attached, it is a method little used in Japan; it also requires much experience with clay, and a great deal of practice.

Rolling the coil, then flattening and stroking it to a concave or lowered center with the tip of the first finger, is an effective and pleasing alternative to pulling—especially when small handles are needed. Whether pulled or rolled and pressed, handles are usually attached with three main strokes at the top, and three at the bottom. First, the points of juncture are scored and moistened. At the top of an open piece, the fingers of the left hand support the handle, while the thumb of the right hand makes a downward lateral stroke on the right side. The motion is away from the center of the coil, in order not to thin and weaken it. Then hands are changed and the left thumb makes its opposing stroke. A third thumb stroke downward below the upper point, where the two preceding strokes have crossed, completes the attachment at the top. The handle is then looped appropriately for the form, and three similar strokes attach the bottom.

The handle is usually wetter than the body of the piece, since the body has often been allowed to stiffen slightly first—especially if the piece has been tooled. The handle and the bottle become one in further drying, however, for the handle, since it is thin and exposed to air from all sides, dries faster than the body. Sometimes the piece must be lightly covered with plastic or placed in a damp box for even drying, and to prevent any cracking between the two pieces.

Lids, too, must be made to fit the piece while it is wet, or else a measurement must be taken, for clay shrinks as it dries. Some refinement in tooling is often needed to relate the two pieces harmoniously. I advise beginners to make several versions of handles and lids for each first effort, so that a discriminating choice can be made.

6

Advanced Lessons

The Renewal of Beginning Forms

The new and more developed pottery modes I will discuss in this chapter in no way replace anything discussed in the last chapter. It is in this sense that pottery is artistic and spiritual, rather than technological. The making of a humble bowl or a wine cup can absorb one's entire powers and often transcend more ambitious projects in depth of meaning. What remains true, however, is that certain basic skills are a prerequisite to others, without reference to the quality that can be achieved in any piece. The lessons of the last chapter never pall, never bore, never get left behind. On the contrary, their very simplicity permits them to be the integrative and meditative path to all that pottery can offer, for through them our insights and sensibilities can be renewed and deepened. Moreover, because the forms of the beginning lessons are small, anonymous, and intimate, they reveal our values and those of our culture all the more.

Largeness

Largeness, though no virtue in and of itself, has its own range of unique qualities. The presence of a beautiful large form commands space and attention. I prefer what I call "humanized largeness," however. Spherical pieces larger than 20 inches (51 cm.) in diameter, for instance, cannot be moved easily. They must be rolled, carted, or lifted by at least two people. I like to be able to hug and carry my pots. The effective scale for me is that of my embrace.

Large pieces do not move through the studio quickly. A series of six or eight big spherical jars may be strewn out in the various processes over a year or more. As I will discuss later, they await finishing until the right moment, like a series of stretched canvases in the painter's studio.

Large Bowls

I do not intend to exhaust the topic of largeness in pottery, but, as in the rest of this book, open up only those processes that I feel are a part of my own work. Since my exposure and concentration have been on the more classical lines of the Great Tradition, and since I have not found these discussed in depth in other books on pottery, this limit through experiential authenticity should not prove restrictive.

To arrive at spherical forms with a 15-inch (38 cm.) diameter or more, using the methods I have learned, one must first master the large bowl. American potters sometimes pride themselves on making large pieces from one mound of clay, but I invariably find pieces crafted in this manner ungainly, unfooted, and unreleased at the base, and out of balance as a result of too much clay on the supporting bottom half. In Arita, large porcelains are made by first fashioning two large hemispherical bowls. I will share with readers this superior method, but first concentrate on the making of a large version of the basic bowl.

Large bowls require a large, wide centering, and a wide opening at the bottom of the cylinder. Pulling the opening out at the base requires much physical strength, as does integrating the thick bottom clay into the cylinder. I often core out the center, using my fingers or, where they cannot reach, a dowel-like rod about 3/4 inch (2 cm.) thick, with a rounded point. This is not done in Arita, but I find that it saves much energy.

To open up without coring, producing a ring instead of a hole, it is possible to work the cylinder wall slowly downward, after opening the top to the depth of the thumbs, by making the thickness of the wall of the opened hole fairly even all around before going lower into the mound. In this way, when the potter approaches maximum depth, he will have already thinned and raised the wall from several progressively lower levels. The top should be kept at a thickness of about 3/4 inch (2 cm.), for the expansion of a cylinder into a wide bowl thins the wall quickly, and too thin a rim warps in firing or cannot be used for joining later onto another bowl for a sphere.

To smooth the bottom of the freshly opened, centered mound, the potter should use a rib that will flatten and spread the clay. A simple, flat edge with a bevel works well. An ideal tool, unknown in America, is the short *nobibera,* a rib used to expand forms upward and outward (see Fig. 8), carved from small green Chinese lilac logs, right into the heart of the grain of the wood. The shape is like that of a large thumb pushing out, except that it is hollowed out so that it has a thickness of no more than 3/8 inch (10 mm.). Like a thumb, it can press down and out equally well. This tool should be no longer than can be comfortably held in the finger span of thumb and fingers, end in the palm, fingertips on the inside curve. The reverse or straight end is ideal for packing, flattening, and widening the inside base of large cylinders. To widen, the nobibera cuts slightly into the wall as the bottom is approached. The hand turns toward the body, or from nine o'clock to six o'clock, against the wheel direction, in this operation.

The vertical thickness left at the bottom of the bowl is usually 3/4 to 1 inch (2 to 2.5 cm.). If the bottom is lower than where the wall can comfortably bow out, either because it is too thin or because the side wall is too thick, a reverse curve effect will appear at the bottom of the

Fig. 8. Short or all-purpose *nobibera* used for large bowls and spheres: 1, side view; 2, front view; 3 marks the breaking point of the curve.

bowl later, where the wall humps up over the outer bump of clay, thus preventing the continuous flow of the hollow. This is a problem needing immediate attention. Use of the nobibera helps prevent this characteristic fault in large bowls.

Next, the cylinder wall must be thinned and integrated, bottom to top, with a choking of the cylinder between each thinning pull. The ideal is a thick (about 3/4 inch, or 2 cm.) but fairly uniform wall with some tapering, so that the bottom may be slightly wider than the top.

After this is achieved, the nobibera can be used to begin the outward pressure against the cylinder's wall, and to continue gradual thinning. Again the wheel goes clockwise. The nobibera rides from the center to the wall, where the "ball of the thumb" of the tool pushes out slightly but firmly against the extended left hand, whose thumb is widely extended so that it acts in a choking fashion as the hands move up the cylinder. The top third of the cylinder is turned out into a noticeable overhang, which keeps reappearing before each new push from the bottom up. It stabilizes the cylinder against wobbling and collapsing under expansion. The next pass up fills in the curve so that the overhang disappears. Then the top third is again pushed out.

At this point, an all-purpose *oshibera,* or pushing rib, comes into play. The outer fingers are now bunched together, thumb behind them, as the wheel turns at very slow speed and the rib slowly pushes the shape out. The rib continues to pull round toward the body and against the wheel direction as it moves from the midpoint of the bottom to the tip of the rim. Pressure at the bottom spring of the curve must be great but contained, for the moving out of the bowl must be gradual and absorbed into the curve above it or the bowl will overhang itself, reverse wall curve at the bottom, and wobble off center or collapse. The outward turning of the top rim or top third precedes each new pass up until only small refinements are made, when a slight outer turning of the rim may suffice. The rim itself is packed with slight downward pressure of the wetted rib between passes, to reinforce it against pulling apart in spreading.

I have presented this process in great detail because it comes from a long tradition unknown to the West. The ideal form for which it strives is that of the cupped hands, made large. In porcelains, the very bottom center of the bowl is left slightly raised, for it will settle down later in firing, and this slight curve will prevent it from becoming too sunken.

Bowls that are not destined to become parts of spheres can retain their parabola-like expansion at the rim. This is often accentuated by flattening out the rim, at the last 1/2 to 1 inch (13 to 26 mm.), to a horizontal out-turn for a lip. This out-turned lip can begin to appear prior to the last several pushes out of the bowl, for it in itself helps stabilize and strengthen the top.

The top rim of bowls that will become parts of large spheres should not have an outward spread; the wall should be straight for a short distance at the top, or else there will be a bump instead of a continuous flow in the curve when the two bowls are joined. It follows also that there is no out-turned horizontal rim in this case.

In Japan, large bowls are thrown on wooden platforms 3/4 to 1 inch (20 to 26 mm.) thick, cut hexagonally to an approximate circular shape, with wooden runners on the bottom measuring 1 × 1 inch (26 × 26 mm.). These platforms are 12 inches (30 cm.) and more in width, as a rule, though they can be of any size (Fig. 9). Platforms from 12 to 18 inches (30 to 46 cm.) in width cover most of my needs for large pots. The platforms are pressed down and leveled flat on a ring of plastic clay about 1 inch (26 mm.) thick and nearly as wide as the length of the runners. (The bottom surface of the runners is wetted before being pressed into the ring.) Fastened as described, the platforms take all the pressure of centering and forming without moving or coming loose.

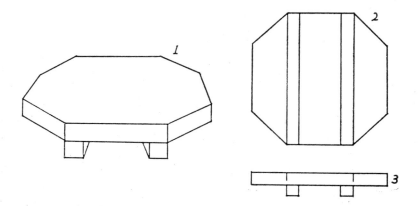

Fig. 9. Wooden throwing platforms: 1, basic representation; 2, bottom view; 3, front end view.

They are very flexible, for they can easily be taken up and moved about the studio. They can also be recentered on a new ring of plastic clay (without rewetting the runners) for any rough or wet tooling desired. I usually cut larger shapes from the platform right after throwing, with a twisted string. They can still be wet-tooled in an upright position after doing this, then later be recut without distorting the bottom. I use a thin guitar string for this second cutting.

Finish tooling of large porcelain and stoneware bowls is done on a chuck, just as for the basic bowl, but obviously a much larger chuck is needed, and it will take assistance from at least one other person to move the bowl easily and safely to the chuck at the proper stage of dryness.

Before doing this, however, I prepare the bowl for finish tooling by placing on it 1/2 inch (13 mm.) of fine clay trimmings. This soaks up moisture and dries out the very bottom so that it is even in dryness with the inside of the bowl. To do this, I flip the bowl over on a circular piece of wood wider than the bowl. The runners of the platforms aid in this process, because they permit the hand to move under the platform so raised. Then I sprinkle the dry trimmings on the bottom of the bowl. It follows that the bowl must be leather hard to take these movements without strain and distortion. While the bottom is drying thus, the whole piece can even be covered with plastic if there is any problem with the rim drying too fast.

To transfer the bowl to the chuck, I usually flip the bowl over onto the extended fingers of my right hand, which holds the inside bottom on top of a pad, like a folded towel, to distribute pressure. Then, while I have the bowl upside down, a helper and I support it, fingers up inside and not just at the rim, and carry it to the chuck. Once cushioned on the chuck, no further help is needed until it is time to remove the bowl, when a reverse of the procedure just described is recommended.

Tooling with regular and curved *kanna,* as required, then occurs, to refine weight and profile before eventually setting the finished foot diameter and hollowing out the bottom inside the foot rim. Sturdy feet are recommended for large bowls. As with smaller bowls and spheres, I bevel out the outer bottom edge of the foot at a 45-degree angle.

At times it is necessary to tool part of the inside bottom of a large bowl to recover a partially lost curve. The ideal, as with the basic bowl, is one of forever expanding openness. It follows that the range of such expansive shapes is extensive. Some bowls approach plates in horizontality. Others deepen through straighter side walls. The former invite interior decoration more than the latter.

Large Spheres

Large spheres are not to be undertaken lightly. The time required to make a large stoneware sphere, from throwing to tooling and slipping, is about five days, with constant attention necessary to the state of the piece. The speed of drying changes according to weather and studio conditions. Extremely fast drying is detrimental to the process, and drying can be slowed down simply by covering the piece with plastic.

I usually throw the top hemisphere or bowl first. Once the desired shape is obtained, with care taken that the curve becomes vertical as it approaches the rim, a ring is then cut through the inside of the bottom with a needle; this will become the open top of the sphere. The cut circle is left in place for now. The upper rim of the bowl is cut on a 45-degree angle with the lower edge on the outside. The bottom hemisphere will be cut on the opposite or complementary 45-degree slope, low side on the inside. Structurally, this assures a tighter join and puts the edges to be healed on inside and outside at different levels. The top half is then cut with a string at the base, and bowl and platform are set aside to dry. Sometimes a bit of wet tooling is done before the pieces are joined. For this, the platform with the bowl on it can be recentered on a fresh ring of plastic clay.

The bottom hemisphere is then thrown. The only difference between it and a regular large bowl is that there is no lip, and the rim has its 45-degree slope. Accurate measurements of diameters are also essential.

Both pieces are allowed to dry to the point where the rims are firm but can still be marked by a fingernail, and where the walls have stiffened sufficiently to bear the weight of the joined hemispheres. Only through practice can the potter judge the appropriate time for joining. Joining too soon or too late leads to problems, such as deformation, splitting, and cracking. I often wet the rims during the drying period, because they tend to dry too fast. The exposed edge may also be wetted and covered with thin plastic.

At joining time, the exposed rim of each piece is carefully scored in a crosshatch fashion. Water is added until a local slip is worked up, which will stay moist during the operation. Another set of hands is needed at the start of the joining process. The top hemisphere, lip well lubricated with slip, is inverted on a wooden circle larger than the bowl's diameter. The entire structure—platform, bowl, wooden disc on top—is turned over at a signal, with one hand of potter and helper on top, the other on the bottom. The inverted bowl is then set down, the platform removed by recutting the base with a guitar string. The circle which was pre-cut by the needle at throwing time is now pushed through.

Four hands now grasp the inverted bowl (or, now, the sphere top) at this opening and lift it from the disc (a foot is often needed to push the wooden disc free from the point of the slipped edge). The top is carried to the waiting bottom, centered on a wheel, edge also slipped, and carefully lowered into place. A difference of 1/16 inches (1.5 mm.) or so at the join will not matter.

Now the potter can take over the work by himself again. Using the all-purpose *oshibera,* with the wheel moving at a slow speed, the inside and outside edges of the join are healed, with bunched finger pressure containing the wall opposite the rib.

The top of the sphere now needs attention. The clay is thicker here than at the join, and wetter. If conditions are right, shoulder, neck, and lip can be changed by rib and finger pressure and by some rewetting. At first it is usually necessary to recut the top area with a needle and, occasionally, cutting tools. Then the thick clay is worked upward, truing the top as it is thinned.

Often there is sufficient clay to make a generous rim or even a neck, or a turret-like small cylinder sitting atop a fully spherical shoulder. The width or mouth size of the sphere is changeable. Many aesthetic decisions need to be made. Simplicity and strength usually win out. A big sphere disdains fancy or thin lips. Stingy openings that both hands and both eyes cannot enter are likewise ruled out. If the sphere is to have a lid, it should be broad and domed.

Often I will bring the clay to the desired shoulder curve and opening diameter and stop. After giving the shoulder several hours to stiffen, I will add several coils and throw an entirely new small cylindrical top and lip. At other times, I will settle for the simplest rolled lip at the edge of the mouth. A soft and rounded feeling is achieved, especially in porcelain, by a more closed mouth which very slightly reverses curve just as it terminates.

Once completed to satisfaction, the sphere is set aside to dry further.

When it can be handled, it is cut free again with guitar string and carefully set, mouth down, on the clay cushion of a large sphere tooling chuck. The bottom is carefully paddled until a concave form occurs. This procedure seems to compact the clay and, coupled with the inner dome effect, allows the bottom to shrink without cracking. In porcelains, and to some degree in stonewares, it prevents the bottom from slumping down in the firing. Then the sphere is turned upright and placed on a thin bed of dry tooling chips. Sometimes it is advisable to use some drying aid for the inner bottom half of a sphere. Lowering in a sixty-watt bulb can be effective; otherwise, time and constant attention, such as covering the sphere with a plastic bag to even out drying, are recommended. The sphere is then tooled with the same self-made *kanna*.

No two spheres ever seem identical to me. The sphere is the most quiet and most universal of forms, a kind of classical metaphor for wholeness, a paradox of simultaneous fullness and emptiness; it is, in a sense, a storage jar for Big Spirit.

The above description is an application of Arita porcelain methods to large stoneware pieces. Most of my large pieces are in stoneware. I do know, however, that there are still further advantages to this process in porcelain, although I have not yet done a series of large spheres in porcelain, mostly because I have not found a porcelain body comparable to the native stone used in Arita.

One of the advantages of using porcelain, however, is that it can be brought back to a state of plasticity, after joining the stiffened hemispheres, by rewetting the clay, waiting, rewetting, and so on. The clay will reach a stage where the entire joined curve can then be pushed out further and in general changed by rib and hand. This is not possible with stoneware, for it will not return to its earlier state in this way.

Large Plates

Large plates need wider feet than large bowls, so platforms of greater diameter are necessary for throwing. I usually roll and thump the mound of clay down, slapping it into a round shape, before taking it to the wheel. The lower and wider the centering, the better. What is needed is a wide expanse before the foot rim, and a wall, shorter than that for a bowl, which is nearly flat and yet still maintains its form in such a daring cantilever. Here the flattened rim or lip which changes curve from the inside is both a structural and aesthetic feature. Structurally, the reverse shape keeps the rim from buckling and slumping. Aesthetically, it pulls the eye horizontally out from the plate's center.

A slightly raised center is recommended for a stoneware plate of wide diameter, since drying and firing will flatten the plate out. Too great a cantilever will cause a similar problem, causing the plate to warp or crack. Uneven setting on a kiln shelf is a further source of distortion in firing.

A 12-inch (30 cm.) foot on a 24-inch (61 cm.) bowl means that there will be a 6-inch (15 cm.) cantilever on each side. Structurally, this is sound. Occasionally, more than one foot rim is used on large plates, but I do not find this as structurally and as aesthetically pleasing as the single foot rim.

In throwing a large plate, the use of the short *nobibera* ensures that the wall of the plate will be pushed out sufficiently, but just short of the final profile. At this point, the all-purpose *oshibera* is used, starting from the very center and moving to the rim, where the reverse, outward pointing lip is set.

As with the bowl, the bottom thickness must be great enough where the wall starts to cantilever so that the clay on the platform will not push up on the wall, causing a reverse curve where the wall and inner base of the plate meet. Some clay on the platform is essential for bracing the wall, but it should be lower than the inside base. Only practice and gradually acquired insight will reinforce what I instruct but can never quite master.

Again help will be needed in placing large plates on the tooling chucks. The process is the same as for large bowls. As with bowls, the bottom is dried out with dry tooling chips, spread out to a depth of about 1/2 inch (13 mm.). Prior to this, some paddling with the rounded canvas-covered paddle can help strengthen the clay against cracking in drying or firing. A sturdy foot rim is recommended for large plates. As with bowls and spheres, I bevel the outside bottom edge of the ring at a 45-degree angle.

Large plates offer beautifully open and full surfaces for decoration, but they bring with them all of the blessings and problems of a circular field. Rings, symmetrical and rhythmic subdivisions, off-center lines, all-over random patterns—there are endless ways into this world. *Winter Sun Screen Plate* (1977; Plate 7) is a favorite of mine. The image came, almost eidetically, from right outside my studio window. A wooden sun screen stood behind a fir tree covered with snow. A curved drift caught the play of shadows through the wooden louvres of the screen. The whole scene, a simple visual poem, translated into black slip on the white ground of a waiting plate, aided by rubber resist stop-out for the edge of the drift and the snow piled on the fir's branches. I would usually not have thought of cutting into a circle with a vertical line like this. Yet the whole works.

Hand and Wheel in Partnership

I do not make a conscious separation of wheel work and hand work. They are one and the same for me. Pottery pinched off the wheel has a center. The spinning of the world and the spinning of the wheel are one. Since I rarely use a motor wheel and work fairly slowly, I never have the feeling that I'm working on a machine. When body, mind, and wheel are one, it is all "hand work."

So by hand work I mean what it not drawn integrally from one piece of clay. The latter depends, after all, on the magic of the wheel. I have already ushered in hand work in discussions of handles and other additions to a basic piece. Still, I will scarcely touch the scope of this subject. Instead I will concentrate on additions that become integral to the wheel. Thus I use the phrase "partnership between hand and wheel." And I will focus on two kinds of such partnership: coiling and throwing, and pinching and stamping.

Already, in discussing large spheres, I have alluded to the addition of coils preparatory to throwing a new top on the shoulder of the sphere. This is a hand-wheel partnership. The coils are thrown and fused into the basic form. But it is equally possible to coil and throw entire pots. This was how the robust undulating jars of the Tamba farmers came into being; so, too, the large water and oil jars of Crete and Shikoku.

My method uses a thrown lower section of the piece as a springboard for subsequent coiling and throwing. The first section must stiffen sufficiently to withstand the weight of coils and the pressures of throwing them once they are added and pinched into place, about three fat coils at a time. The coils are rolled to a thickness of about 1 inch (26 mm.) thick; they are alternately rolled and rhythmically tweaked to lengthen them. Then each coil is carried to the wheel, fed into place with the left hand and pinched as it goes on with the right hand. The coils are fused carefully with the fingers, and then pinched upward slightly, choking in by the pressure of the hands toward each other as if squeezing a section of the wall together. Any bumps on the wall are smoothed out, inside and out, with a rib (the all-purpose *oshibera* is ideal). After this, the wall is slipped and the new section is thrown upward, continuing the desired shape.

At the juncture of drier and wetter clay there will probably be a slight bump, but this is characteristic of coiled and thrown forms. The bump can be worked out of the outside by scraping and later tooling, but there is a certain honesty of expression in leaving it.

The wall is left to dry again, and then the entire process is repeated. This procedure is somewhat like projecting a reinforced concrete bridge over a chasm, bit by bit, except that in the case of a pot, verticality and gravity are conquered. Pots of great scale can be made by this method. I have made bottles and cylinders over 40 inches (1 meter) high (Plate 8).

If desired, pits and hollows can be filled with clay, then smoothed with a stiff metal-toothed scraper; however, the subtle departures from absolute symmetry of curve and straight line fit this process, and have their own aesthetic character. Some of my large cylinders, for example, were inspired by the subtle asymmetrical growth of the trunks of palm trees. I have also used hand coiling and throwing to extend the middle section between two hemispheres, keeping the top hemisphere damp while waiting for the coiled and thrown section to stiffen. An elongated jar is the result (Plate 9).

The second method of coiling begins in the same way as the one just described, but only one coil at a time is added, and it is not pinched into place in the wall curve but bent inward, not upward, as in throwing. Then a process I call "stamping" is begun. In this, a bisque stamp, usually around an inch in diameter and bearing an appropriate image, such as a wave form, is used on the outside of the piece while finger pressure is exerted on the inside of the wall right opposite it. Each pinch of fingers and stamp stretches the wall, and this expansion must be taken into account as part of the form. When I first tried this method on a large sphere, I could not get it to terminate, for it would not close in. I have now mastered this art to a fair degree. It requires bending the coil inward to horizontal position before pinching and stamping.

The pinching-stamping rhythm is patient, regular, and strong. I typically use only a portion of a bisque stamp, overlapping one press with the next, while inside a noticeable hollow finger hole is left behind. The wall thus pinched and stamped becomes a strong and thin corrugated surface, the design of finger and stamp an integral part of the building process. The wall is so strong that it can be teased in and out with finger pressure below the point where one is working, thus allowing correction and continuity to the form.

Great patience is required, for there is a lot of surface to be covered in a large spherical form. One feels more like an architect than a wheel potter, although building the piece thus on the wheel from a thrown base section keeps the feeling of the wheel always in the background. In fact, the foot is involved in a slow turn as the pinching and stamping travels around the piece.

When new coils are added, the stamping fuses right across the join. Again, drying cycles are necessary between coiled and stamped sections of about 10 inches (25 cm.) in height. The pinched and stamped wall, however, dries or "sets up" sooner than the coiled and thrown wall.

Pieces made by this process have a timeless and primitive feeling (Plate 10). In Karatsu, near Arita, a similar method is used with the sandy local stoneware clay; however, a carved and curved wooden anvil is held by the left hand inside the piece while a carved flat wooden paddle strikes against it from the outside. The result is similar. The clay expands and becomes imprinted by the building process itself.

Working in Porcelain

In one sense, by identification and influence, my work is a blend of two traditions—the mingei, or folk art, tradition mediated for me through the lives and influence of Bernard Leach and Shoji Hamada, and the Arita tradition. But it is the porcelain tradition of Arita as received from my teacher, Manji Inoue, that has taught me the meaning of perfection through discipleship to a living tradition. Through me and the passage of time, a unification of these two influences has been at work. Many of the methods I discuss and teach are my own peculiar fusion of the two, concentrating largely on stoneware, but extending and modifying the porcelain methods and disciplines. The logic of a fusion such as this is as much autobiographical as culturally necessitated. I also reason, however, that the common and the refined, the high and the low, revitalize each other.

The spirit of porcelain brings a certain clarity, purity, and classicism to the fore. These qualities spread and fuse into the use of a humble native clay as well. Porcelain invites precision and preciousness, but it can be imbued with robustness and breadth and ease of statement as well.

The superiority of porcelain traditions of hand and tool is clear to me. The sensuous feel and responsiveness of porcelain is unparalleled. Though delicate, porcelain is tougher than the strongest stoneware. Porcelain will swell further, change direction quicker, and respond to a lyrical touch more sensitively than any other clay I know.

The simple bowl form described in chapter 5, and the methods for its formation in stoneware, were an adaptation of the beginning porcelain discipline; the spirit of the two is much the same. The porcelain bowl method differs in that the *nobibera* is introduced in the first step, after the ball is opened and the opened cylinder is choked upward on the stem. The nobibera used here is longer (about 10 in.; 26 cm.) than the 5-inch (13 cm.) nobibera used in large bowls and spheres described earlier in this chapter. The shapes are much the same, however.

The 10-inch nobibera is grasped firmly in the right hand (after the edges of nobibera and porcelain cylinder have been covered with slip) and pressed gently downward at the very center of the spinning cylinder (with the wheel now moving clockwise). The center is felt at the tip and a beautiful rounded surface forms. The left hand encircles the stem beneath the bowl, the stem between the little and third finger. This hand presses up gently as the nobibera presses down. The left hand then moves upward, against the wall backed by the nobibera, which slowly turns against the wheel direction. The extended fingers of the left hand move up the wall of the forming bowl while the nobibera stays in place, apart from its slow turn into the wheel direction. Near the top third of the bowl thus raised, the nobibera is turned to create a right angle with the wall of the bowl and the left-hand fingers and nobibera together move up to thin and finish the rim of the bowl.

In principle, then, the process is the same, but reversed from the stoneware adaptation. In the latter, the inside hand moves at first, while the outside hand shapes and remains still. In porcelain, the outside hand moves first, while inside the nobibera shapes and remains still. In both cases, both hands move together to finish the wall.

The shape arrived at by tool and hand in porcelain eludes description. Its rightness is all in the feel of the movements, as in stoneware, but the fineness of porcelain and the shaping ability of the nobibera are a unique partnership in throwing.

Other stages in the creation of the basic porcelain bowl are similar to those described for stoneware. Porcelain workers will often, however, cut bowls free while they are spinning. To do this, they take a length of finely twisted cord of about 20 inches (51 cm.) that has a knot at one end. With the wheel spinning clockwise, this knot is held in the left hand; then, addressing the stem at the tweak from the front, the string is pulled taut. After the string touches the tweak, the knot-end is released. Still parallel to the tweak, the string is allowed to go around once and overlap itself. Then, with a smooth but quick jerk of the right hand, the bowl is severed. The knot locks at the overlap and a smooth cut is effected. Mastery of this technique takes much practice; it represents a further refinement and economy in the "dance" of the basic bowl. Skilled Arita potters will often even remove the bowl with the V of the spread middle fingers of both hands, palms up, while the wheel is still spinning.

Porcelain can recover its plastic state after wet tooling, whereas in stoneware, the drying process is irreversible. Dry forms can be joined by working up a penetrating local slip at the join only. Thus the severe and stately forms of a Chinese wine ewer or incense burner are possible.

Porcelain responds to pressed designs, to carving, to paddling and reshaping in a manner mind-boggling to a stoneware potter. Take, for example, the production of a large *hana-bachi,* or bowl shaped like a flower. The bowl is first wet tooled, then it is carefully wetted at six equal intervals around the circumference. The wetting is localized to several inches (about 5 cm.) running from rim down the outside toward the foot, and it is repeated until the six areas so wetted respond to finger pressure. The finger presses inward (by point pressing only, not by a sliding pressure, which disturbs the clay surface and leads to cracks) until strong indentations at the top fuse into disappearing identations further down the wall surface. Next, the inside of the indentation is scored and wetted, then a coil is added, then slowly fused, by scraping away with a bamboo blade, until a sharp edge appears on the inside. The outside inmost part of the indentation is then also sharpened up with the same bamboo scraper. Later on, finish scraping will unify all working marks into the piece.

Still later, before bisquing, the piece is rubbed down with a folded pad of old sheeting, dipped in water, and wrung out. This pad is moved in circular fashion over the surface to seal and refine it, by bringing the very finest grains to the top. As soon as slip clogs the sheeting, it must be rinsed and wrung out clean. A similar process is used on all fine porcelains in Arita before bisquing, except for those with carved designs or for finger-shaped ceremonial tea bowls. Porcelain surfaces so rubbed have a satiny surface, even where unglazed.

Since I will describe carved designs on porcelains in chapter 7, I will not go into much detail here, except to point out the beauty of direct carving on porcelain, left as its only embellishment. One of my favorites among my own porcelains, in contrast, has nothing on it but a clear porcelain glaze, so that it stands out in all its classic white radiance.

Porcelain takes on raised designs with equal success. I have tried versions of the French *pate sur pate* method of building up a design from porcelain slip, brush stroke over brush stroke. I have also used a fine cake decorator's nozzle in the same way, extruding a thin bead on the slightly dampened porcelain surface.

The reverse effect is also possible. A wet brush can play over hard edges and dissolve them away. Such an approach is also useful near joints of handles, knobs, necks, and the like.

The method described for the *hana-bachi* form is applicable elsewhere as well. I have used it for indentations on a bottle and, as well, for squaring off a bottle. In the latter case, as with the inside edge of the fluting on the *hana-bachi,* a coil can be added, in this instance to create a sharp right-angled corner to the squared-off edges at the middle of the bottle, which retains its contrasting rounded top and bottom.

I feel certain that my preference for stonewares slipped in white has come from the decorative and glazing clarity natural to porcelain. To be sure, stoneware traditions the world round do so as well, but in my own case I feel a stoneware spirit parallel to that of porcelain.

Plain porcelain glazes, without decorations or coloring oxides, will still reflect a great range of subtle differences from firing. Examples of the same glaze used on the same batch of porcelain clay will educate one's sensitivities to this subtle and quiet range of noble restraint.

I have only touched on the world of porcelain, as befits my openness to its wonders. But something of its spirit, its methods, and its tradition pervades all else I present.

7

Decorating

Taste and Fashion

On or off the wheel, pottery stands forth as a timeless symbol of integration and unity. The dialectic of wholeness of body-mind precedes and follows practice. Modern man's hubris as maker has distorted the values of tradition and discipleship. Terms such as decorative arts, minor arts, crafts as opposed to arts, artisans as opposed to craftsmen, and functional as opposed to art pottery reflect the vanity and the pejorative tone of our labels. Nowhere is this more apparent than in decorating. In origin, however, the words "decorate," "decorative," and "decoration" retain their root meanings: to be fitting and acceptable.

Further inquiry shows the need to set off taste from fashion in our effort to delimit the meanings of decorating. Simply put, taste and decoration are not subservient to ruling fashion. Taste projects an ideal community. "[It] makes an act of knowledge ... which cannot be separated from the concrete situation on which it operates and cannot be reduced to rules and concepts," according to Hans-Georg Gadamer, a contemporary Western philosopher who studied this problem for many years.[1] An evaluation and judgment of something is necessary to see how fitting it is in relation to a whole. This requires the development of an intuitive sense, a thinking-in-action, which trusts the living wisdom of the unified body-mind.

So it is with decorating. One cannot demonstrate decoration; one can only decorate. As in all creation, the thought and the act clash in the birth of the new; thus neither all thought nor blind action will suffice.

Levels of Decoration

"Accidents" are not decorative unless they "fall toward" (to use the original meaning) the event or happening of decorating. Kiln accidents, as in wood firing, or as in an old Tamba pot fired in an *anagama* (where part of the natural clay roof often falls on the pot), are decorative because they are linked directly to the process of firing. Such accidents are indeed natural happenings. As such, all pots fired in high-fired kilns with active flame in the chamber receive degrees of accidental or natural decoration (see the zigzag firing crack on the Jomon period [10,000 to 300 B.C.] earthenware jar, Plate 11). As we link our knowledge and intention with such natural processes we enter into a dialogue in which we speak the first word and the kiln speaks the last.

Thus the accidents of natural decoration (which are never purely accidental) are the basis for our attitude toward all decoration. Some potters settle for the subtlety of accidental, natural decoration alone. This is the humblest route to follow, as long as we do not take it up in fear. Participating fully in the natural process of firing as decorating requires the responsible dialectic of thought-action.

But even the earliest potters did not rely solely on firing as decoration. The scratch of a twig, the impress of the forefinger, the partially healed coil, the effigy on the rim of the bowl, the legs that became a representation of feet—these and more appear from the earliest times in clay.

Many of these forms of decoration I would call the second level of accident—the spontaneity of the making. Whenever we leave a mark on a pot we form a near-symbol, if not already a symbol. We intend what we do, or, if not, what we have done forms our intention. When I am constructing a pot by a combination of throwing, coiling, and pinching with fingers and a bisque stamp, forming and decorating are one. It is only when we arrive at the third level and pick up a brush or a carving tool that disciplines and strategy make their appearance—even where technique and patterns come into play. Here is where we get into problems and where we risk ruining many pots.

The third level of accidental or natural decoration is hardest to learn because it ceases being accidental or natural for many of us. Yet it is at this level that we can play simultaneously with levels one and two. The accidents of firing and making must be fused with whatever intentional decoration we take up on the third level. The integrity and presence of a great pot often depend on the organic fusion of all three levels. To these we can add an intimation of those still higher levels of the spirit opened up as well on the third level, as the whole world of man's symbols and images come into potential and poetic being. A pot of Hamada's that I hold as I write unifies the fire and glaze, the making and tooling, the slipping and spontaneous brush decoration, and this is all projected still further by its living weight in relation to my eye and body, its "command performance" in my own hands. Were I to use it in the daily ritual of eating, it would participate as well in the everyday sacred, and transcend its position as an aesthetic object.

Disciplined Spontaneity

The practitioner of a traditional art in the East—in truth, anyone who inhabits a meaningful and living discipline—opens himself or herself up for trained spontaneity. The very word "art" carries the connotation of spontaneity. The hand finds the form in moving and the form moves the hand in coming into being. Gadamer states this concept more abstractly:

> [The] work of art is play . . . its actual being cannot be detached from its representation and . . . in the representation the unity and identity of a structure emerge . . . an entity that exists only by always being something different is temporal in a more radical sense than everything that belongs to history. It has being only in becoming and in return.[2]

So again the image of relaxed concentration, of serious play, is evoked. The cook knows his or her seasonings intuitively. The potter who lives around the making and firing of pots is always decorating—that is, trying to locate what is fitting, elegant, and disciplined. Discipleship is the way of decorating; it is not something added onto something else. Organic, living decoration is like sentiment appropriate to the occasion. The two stoneware incense boxes shown in Plate 12, one by Hamada, the other by Kanjiro Kawai, demonstrate the potters' reliance on discipleship, partly through their repetition of beloved brush strokes on simple, yet charming, shapes.

How is spontaneity trained? By discipleship, native exuberance and vitality, playful repetition, forgetfulness, and risk. And especially by life-relatedness. Decoration is celebration. It commemorates a life-art connection. It decorates the event. A sentiment, a poem, the name of person, place, or event, become directly transformed into art and decoration. I was originally a painter, and though that identification continues to open me up toward image and symbol, what I do in decorating pots is a world apart. What is painted, scratched, or carved on pots is never painting, graphics, or sculpture, but a transformation into a new structure that echoes the problem of architecture yet is different from that too. For one thing, as I have hinted, the accidents of the third level, intentional decoration, must remain subordinate to or in relation to fire and forming, the first and second levels of decoration.

Two Poles of Spontaneity: Containment and Dispersion

I see two large modes or moods of decoration: spontaneity with containment and spontaneity with dispersion, two poles that exploit the lyrical and calligraphic on the one hand, and the symphonic and architectonic on the other. Either mode can take up the commemorative-poetic form and symbol drawn directly from one's life-world or turn toward archaeology of past art. Either mode can also take up the abstract, and with a more geometric or a more organic bias. And cutting across both modes can be one of three attitudes: going with, going against, or ignoring the form or context of the pot. Further, the pot as round and near symmetry, can be received as open symbol for the universe, or as reflective of its structural complexity. In one case we have deep, ethereal, oceanic space: the space of nothingness that can be pierced by the song of a bird, the quiet of a soft breeze on a cloudless night, or a heroic deed. In the other case, we have the strata and separations that complicate the structure of each organic whole: the detailed complexity of organic nature, the symphonic harmony of a landscape by Rubens, Monet, or Bonnard.

In short, one might say that the decorations of pots can be all that we can be. But there are affinities. Spontaneity by containment prefers the space of nothingness in which the undivided lyrical event can occur. The moment will decide whether it will go with, against, or ignore the form. This is a fast-burning qualitative immediate present. All hangs on the immediate balance, and the scales are delicate. This is the act of heroes. Best to have the right form and brush and atmosphere. The strategic power must be encircled (or contained) by the forces of spirit. Two pots that immediately come to mind as superb examples of spontaneity by containment are the black stoneware spheres by American potter Lawrence Jordan, shown in Plate 13. Technically, nothing could be simpler: Black clay, with sufficient sand and fireclay in it, is thrown, wet tooled, then tooled finally again when dry, to impart the grainy varied surface texture *in,* not on, these forms. Then, at the right moment, a single stroke or two of white slip sings across this sphere-as-universe, breathing life into it. A calligraphy of liquid motion falls upon the form in an unrepeatable timeless moment. A mist of ash glaze falls on the top part of the sphere (after the bisque fire), fusing imperceptibly with the clay and white slip but ending no one knows where, just barely sealing the textured surface.

These forms absorb the light and create a space around them, like fine sculptures. They naturalize the place where they rest.

Spontaneity by dispersion separates out the unity by refraction and diffraction into its ten thousand components. It suspends these in the vital medium of life and space. Spontaneity by dispersion is a slow-burning, trusting, nurturing qualitative immediate present. The qualitative immediate present is all that man knows of eternity, so why not draw it out lovingly? If one lyrical passage is good, ten are better. One break in the mood and the complicated fabric of forms becomes busy work. All hangs on the extended balance, and in such interplays of theme and variation the scales are also delicate. This is the act of the tellers of epics. Best to have the right place and audience. The strategic power must be rhythmically distributed and apportioned by the forces of a unified spirit. For the ten thousand things are not one thing after another, but ten thousand things as one. The one and the many are the same universe. Containment and dispersion both reflect the spirit alive in the qualitative immediate present. (See Plate 14, hexagonal porcelain vase by Masashi Sakaida of the Kakiemon studio. Here we find a sparing but rich use of color, including the *kaki* [persimmon] red for which the Kakiemon studio is world famous, and from which the studio name springs. In this vase, opposite faces in the six sides repeat the floral motif. Again, opposing qualities unite, for this vase is restrained and precious; it connotes distinctive refinement, joyful elegance.)

The clay, the workplace, the wheel, the brush, the colored clay, the kiln are a part of decoration, for they inform the spirit of the present even as we empower them to do so. This black slip complicated by a dozen natural materials intuitively combined is crucial to a range of rich quiet tones. This ash glaze, applied just so, preserved in part from a stock years old, is crucial to the stony fusion of the accidents of decoration from fire, forming, and intentional surface enrichment. This kiln and the synchronicity of weather and attitude are crucial to the postponed judgment of the spiritual unity preceding and following the event of firing. So seen, decoration is not just what is fitting to the whole. Decoration *is* the whole. It is not even finished at the firing. Now it is the attunement of life and pot in the right environment and attitude. Thus we can speak of an ecology, not just a technique, of decoration. I might share three admonitions supportive of this attitude: Make no comparisons, make no judgments, and give up your need to understand with the mind alone.

Finally, at the most profound level, vital decorations come unsought. They stand out from events otherwise insignificant and meaningless were it not for a fertile readiness within our own imaginative world. The sight of trees on winter fields, for example, first caught out of the corner of the eyes while out driving, can leap directly onto a jar covered with white slip, waiting patiently back in the studio. (See Plate 15, *Trees on Winter Fields.*) This 16-inch (40 cm.) jar had been previously coated, *hakeme* style, with scrubbed layers of plastic white slip. I divided it into two large horizontal zones by means of three double-lined divisions, at shoulder-neck, the high part of the belly, and toward the foot. These divisions, going with the form, stabilized it for the wandering field-row divisions, which formed a network over the whole sphere, but never cut through the encircling bands. Against these snow-field grounds the tracery of the varied trees and bushes appeared, painted in black slip.

Details of Decorating

The topic of decorating, in addition to its primary aesthetic and philosophical bases, has its procedural and quasi-technical ones. While it is procedures that I will discuss in this section, my viewpoint is never completely technological, since holism of body-mind through immersion in discipleship to tradition is the grand theme of this book.

In line with this, I am not writing an exhaustive compendium. Thus, although I have explored salt glazing and wood firing in depth, I will not present them here; the same applies to raku, overglaze enamels, and lustres. Other books take up these important aspects of the potter's art.

My discussion of decorating techniques applies to high-fire stoneware and porcelain, and to kilns with active flame in their chambers (gas and oil kilns, down-draught and up-draught, natural and forced draught). Since the clay body itself is a basic part of all decorating, I will refer to the range that I know: native stoneware clay used direct from the ground, native clay plus blended mine clays, blended mine clays for stoneware, and blended porcelain. Within stoneware itself, there is the range from a plastic, fine-grained clay with little sand or fireclay, to a raku-like clay, where ball clay, sand, and fire clay appear in equal parts. This full range of clays is the keyboard on which I play. It ties all decorating in directly with the accidents of forming and firing.

In decorating, I have a bias toward the natural side: direct painting, carving, and resist. Decorating can occur, depending on the method, at wet, dry, and bisque stages (bisque is ceramic ware that has been fired once, without glaze).

Direct Painting

Slips, stains, and underglaze blue (or *gosu,* as the material used on Japanese blue-and-white porcelains is called) constitute my materials for direct painting, with an emphasis on slips. These require differing applications, so I will discuss them separately.

Since slips are heavy in plastic clay—especially those used on damp ware—they do not act like paints in their application. Not only are they often different in unfired, fired, and glazed versions, but they also have a weight and character that requires brushes and methods of painting unique to them. Slips are more laid on than painted on. The best brushes are those with long bristles—neither too hard nor too soft—that will hold a good quantity of slip. The viscosity of the slip is also important. It cannot be too runny nor too thick.

White slips benefit from repeated or layered applications. This is especially true for the textured or *hakeme* damp white slip application. I often use hakeme white on large spheres (15 inches; 38 cm. or more in diameter), applying it right after finish tooling of the damp ware. I like the texture on these expansive forms as a ground for later decoration. Glazing and overspraying of stains picks up this texture in subtle ways in the glaze firing. In *Winter Flock Vase* (Plate 16), a black slip decoration of birds and trees against the sky was painted directly on top of a white hakeme ground. The texture of the ground adds atmosphere to the painted decoration.

The application of hakeme white slip on damp ware requires the appropriate slip (for damp only) and careful application. While scrubby direct application has its own beauty, I usually apply two or three coats, waiting several minutes to half an hour between each coat. Right after the application of the last coat, I immediately load more slip on with a rough, self-made brush of wheat or broom straw bound together. The dripping and running slip is distributed in all directions over an area by the brush until it starts to set slightly, when the final swirling or raised texture is imprinted on it. Only a partial area of a large form can be handled at one time, so that as that area is extended the passages between them must be fused with longer strokes. I usually do the bottom of the sphere first, with the pot upside down on its lip or held in a chuck.

Plate 17 shows a fine illustration of the direct hakeme style. Made by Shoji Hamada, this salt-glazed rectangular bottle is vigorously decorated, first with a ground of white slip applied hakeme style with a stiff brush of wheat or broom straw so that individual strokes of the scrubby brush show and overlap each other. Four direct strokes were made, like ascending arches or waves. Secondly, it is decorated by a large version of the same basic but ever-varied Hamada brush motif. This time it is done so quickly and so large that it breaks right over the shoulder of the bottle (as partially does the hakeme white slip beneath it). The loose vitality of hakeme and brush design, expansive as they both are, soften and humanize the harsh boxiness of the bottle form. The bottle almost becomes a quiet frame for the brush performance.

The rest of the bottle is a quiet speckled tan brown, slightly varying at edges as is the nature of a vapor glaze. The quietness of the glaze and the color it brings to the background, here the entire bottle, is a perfect foil for the strength and vitality of Hamada's hakeme and iron-brushed design.

Another piece that sums up much of the Hamada spirit and puts direct slip painting to good use seen in Plate 17—Hamada's stoneware bowl, 4 1/2 inches high, 7 1/8 inches diameter (11 cm./18 cm.). The upper outside of this freely thrown, tooled, and decorated bowl is unevenly brushed with a blue-gray slip. The very rim is generously dipped in a thick kaki slip glaze. Where the tooled plane meets the untooled top half of the bowl, there is an uneven band of the flesh tone which appears on the entire inside of the bowl. Thus four color ranges set off the outside from the inside: the curdly gray of glaze on tooled surface, the fleshy tone of glaze on untooled surface, the blue-gray slip, the kaki slip glaze at the rim.

Cutting across the first three of these on two faces of the bowl is Hamada's favorite brush design, in iron, from deep to translucent brown. A tiny splash of the blue-gray slip penetrates the inside bowl below the kaki rim, suggesting the abandon with which it must have been applied. Throwing lines are apparent on the inside, from the spiral at the bottom center to the top rim. These impart another subtle visual and tactile vitality to the whole. They appear on the outside, on the top untooled portion as well.

Stains are effective, but since they are made almost completely of coloring oxides, their color is much more intense, and they are usually diluted, and used in watercolor fashion. Stains can also be mixed with slips, especially white slip, for subtle tints and shades. (Similarly, white slip can dilute a basic black, red, or blue slip.) By using a white slip appropriate to wet, dry, or bisque stages, these tints and shades cover a wide range of uses.

The basic red and black slips I list later in this chapter can be used at wet, dry, and bisque stages; they can also be used over the applied glaze on bisque, with care taken to apply a thinner coat of slip on non-damp surfaces. (Over powdery glazes, it's often necessary to brush on gum tragacanth solution, to protect the piece from smudging.)

Underglaze *gosu* blue is most often used on porcelain, and usually for direct painting on porcelain bisque, but it is equally effective on stoneware and on dry or partially damp ware (see Plate 19). Since brush application to the bisque requires a steady and practiced hand, I am more inclined to apply gosu to a piece before firing, using a sgraffito approach (to be described later).

Gosu and stains both allow a range of washes and densities, but a problem they share is a tendency to smudge more readily than slips. Isolating sprays of gum tragacanth solution will protect a piece for moving.

Even with slips, smudging can occur. Large forms should be carefully wrapped in a blanket and taped tightly for carrying them about the studio, for handling while swirling glaze on their interiors, or for moving sprayed, glazed bisque pots to the kiln for the glaze firing.

Resist Methods

The resist technique consists of stopping out certain portions of a clay piece so that slips or glazes applied to the piece will adhere only where there is no resist substance. I use two basic resist materials: heated wax and latex rubber. Paraffin and kerosene in equal proportions make up the wax base: The paraffin is melted, then removed from the heat and an equal proportion of kerosene poured in. For safety, a double boiler that completely covers the hot plate head is advisable, or better still an enclosed element pan or crock where the wax cannot be ignited by an exposed heat source.

This wax mix melts easily and sets up quickly in use. It will not ruin brushes, since they can be cleaned easily—immersed in kerosene, then washed with soap and warm water. I use several brushes interchangeably for slips and wax resist.

The beauty of wax resist is its breadth and spontaneity. It invites freely brushed passages. These often fade out into textures as the wax cools and the brush runs out of wax, so a stroke will show a full and a textured end. Drips and drops are also characteristic of wax resist, so the effect is often that of a very freely executed batik (see Plate 20, *Homage to Hokusai*).

I prefer long-hair, full-bodied brushes for wax resist. Most of these I make myself, from dog hair (the hackles from the back of a dog's neck are best) and horse tail. These brushes are thin and long, from 4 to 8 inches (10 to 20 cm.) in hair length; they invite very spontaneous lines because they droop under their wax load and so must actually be slung through the air against gravity to be applied.

I also have a fat deer-tail Japanese brush about 3 inches (8 cm.) long and 1 inch (2.6 cm.) thick at the large end, which comes down to a perfect point. This brush is actually a *dami fude*, a brush used to float lighter washes of gosu blue onto bisque porcelain in Japan (see Plate 21), but I find it excellent for wax resist, since it will drip or paint thin lines and make vigorous strokes when pressure is increased.

Though I occasionally apply wax resist on dry greenware, burning off the wax in the bisque kiln, I more commonly do wax resist over glazed bisque pieces. Lately I have used almost exclusively two simple glazes—an ash glaze and a Shino glaze. Shino glazes are made up almost completely of feldspar, and are so powdery that pieces must be sprayed or brushed with a gum tragacanth solution before applying the wax.

Plate 23 shows Japanese potter Kyusetsu Miwa's skillful use of the Shino glaze on a square stoneware bottle about 11 inches (28 cm.) high. One upper shoulder corner, part of the side, and a portion of the neck and lip of the bottle were dipped in a dark red-brown, thickish, dry-surfaced slip (where exposed). The entire piece is glazed with a thick, curdled Shino glaze, which breaks and crawls back to reveal the base clay and the corner with the dark slip. The random pattern of these breaks is a distinctive feature of the Shino tradition.

The uneven character of the glazing further accentuates this style. Milky drips and beads, thick and thin splashes, appear as left, for this stiff glaze has solidified just on the verge of fusing, like water transformed suddenly into ice. On the two sides adjacent to the face shown here, perfect arches from the fingers holding the piece upside down for glazing appear right where the walls join the foot—two finger arches on one side, one on the other. The toasty, orangish clay body bleeds through the thinly glazed areas in the brighter red-orange tones common to prized Shino tea bowls. A luminous pinkish cast permeates even the thickly glazed areas.

When I apply slips over a wax resist decoration, I thin them with water so that they function more like stains. Often I break up the slip colors so that not just one hue permeates the whole piece. One way of doing this is to brush on several inches of one color, say a red slip, and then change to a different color to cover the next area, say a blue or black slip. Another common approach involves thinning a stain to a dilute wash and covering the entire piece with it. The area close to and overlapping the wax can then be touched up with fuller-strength stain and a smaller, more easily controlled brush. The whole process is free and moving. Drips and gradations add to the life of the piece.

Wax resist must usually be liberally used, so that lighter design areas are not engulfed by an excess of dark over-brushing. An alternative method, where less resist is applied, limits the brushed stain or slip to the region of the designs only, not covering the entire pot.

Rubber latex resist permits other painterly effects. It is usually applied with more care and precision than wax, which, in itself changes the character of the designs. Straight or clean edges and forms are typical of rubber resist. Since it can easily be removed (it can be picked up like a large rubber band), sequential effects are possible. For example, an area can be stopped out with rubber, a background color washed over the forms, the rubber pulled off, and details painted within the stopped-out areas (see Plate 22, *Snow Pine Jar*). I also use rubber for delicate lines and bands on a piece, since a brush can be run freely over the edge. All that will appear later is the part of the stroke that hit the clay.

Rubber is hard on brushes, and it is advisable to wash them out frequently while doing extended designs (if soap is scrubbed into the bristles, then squeezed out, the rubber will not adhere to the bristles as much during application).

Sgraffito

Sgraffito is equivalent to a scratch-board method, where a pointed or loop instrument cuts through a top layer of color to a bottom, base, or body color. Although the scratching is usually done through a slip darker than the body, it can also be done through a slip lighter than the body. (I sometimes stain the grooves of scratches through white slip, on the bisque, sponging off excess surface stain, before glazing the piece. The result has some of the effect of an etching.)

Designs can be linear or a combination of line and mass, with the background color more or less scraped out at places. One of my favorite methods is to apply black slip to a damp piece. When the surface is dry to the touch but still damp within, I begin direct carving with a fine wire-loop tool or a carving *kanna*. No matter how large the piece, it must usually be carved at one sitting, so it doesn't dry out. Even so, it may be necessary to use the plant-misting sprayer, to revive some areas and keep chipping at a minimum.

Another approach especially appropriate to a fine surface, as in porcelain, is to apply a wash of underglaze *gosu* blue to the still damp wet-tooled pot, which is then carved with the self-made carving *kanna* (Fig. 2, page 57). Great detail is possible with these materials and tools (see Plate 24, *River Landscape Vase*).

The detail on stoneware through black slip is rougher and more robust (see Plate 25, lidded box). If an ash glaze is sprayed on such pieces later, it is a good idea, halfway through the spraying, to rub the glaze into the grooves with fingertips, filling them and making them lighter in tone.

The whitish ash glaze listed at the end of this chapter combines subtly and quietly with black slip sgraffito. The slip comes through with a range of tones and colors—black, brown, tan, and a quiet blue—while the grooves pick up an off-white to tan color. The Shino glaze listed also combines well with sgraffito through white slip, where stain has first been rubbed into the grooves.

As with resist methods, especially where dark slips or stains are used, it is advisable to do considerable sgraffito carving to prevent the piece from becoming heavy and dark. Less carving or scratching is required when a slip lighter than the body is used.

I have achieved some striking results using both resist and sgraffito methods on a very dark clay body. In these cases, the body underneath will usually stain somewhat through the lighter slip applied over it. The whitish ash glaze works best over such dark clay bodies.

It is also possible to do surface scratches directly on a piece without applying any slip whatsoever, but this I will discuss under carving below. Korean potters rub or brush white slip into the grooves cut on a piece, then scrape the whole piece to leave an inlaid white line. Another technique I have tried with success is to apply white and black slips adjacent to each other on a damp piece. After these have dried slightly, I carve into the white and into the black with a fine wire-loop cutter, deep enough so that an actual coil or string of the colored slip is removed. The white coil is then inlaid into the dark groove, and the dark coil into the white groove, and the surface is later paddled to insure a tight fit. The result is that of a primitive inlaid design.

Carving

Japanese potters use self-made *kanna* with tiny cutting ends to carve designs into porcelain. This method probably originated in ancient China and was passed to Japan by way of Korea.

The carving kanna is made from the same strap or banding metal mentioned for the tooling kanna (page 57). The end is tapered to mid-point of the shaft, but it terminates in a small keystone-like form (see Fig. 2) instead of a point. This end form is filed on the edges to a 45-degree angle, then bent at a right angle. The innermost sharp corner of this tool will cut a groove with a steeper and shallower side, thus giving a shaded form that has been used to perfection on older porcelains, especially Oriental celadons (where the grooves darken from the pooled glaze).

This carving kanna should be used when the clay is nearly leather hard, but wet enough so that a slightly raised burr is produced when the clay is cut. If the clay is too wet, the tool will clog; too dry, and the line will shatter at the edges. It may be used on damp porcelain and stoneware alike, either straight on the piece or, as in sgraffito, through slip, stain, or *gosu* blue. It makes a strong, vital, and clear line or sets off a clean form. The carving kanna is also effective for bas relief carving, especially of grainy clays (see Plate 26). In the latter case, the outline is isolated and set down, then the background carved away.

Raised Applied Designs

Over the years I have created space divisions and forms by the addition of thin coils of clay as a three-dimensional "drawing" medium. Just recently I completed a covered jar on which lines suggestive of hills become space divisions, which in turn are ground for trees, fences, flowers, plants, and other landscape elements, all through the use of raised coils. The lid carries through this same spatial and figurative interplay. The coils must be attached with slip at the proper stage of dampness of the piece. It is advisable as well to fuse the coils with their ground through finger pressure and a rounded stick, which seals and rounds the attaching point.

This slow and patient method has its peculiar aesthetic merits, and the positive effect of simplifying and clarifying form. Details, while possible, are limited in quantity and therefore force a choice among alternative possibilities. As in much decoration, and as in the discipleship of the Great Tradition in general, what limits is what frees. Acceptance of limitation is a dawning wisdom which allows spontaneous poetry to arise like the wind.

Stamping and Pinching

The surface of a piece can be three-dimensionally decorated by pinching the clay wall between inside fingers and an outside bisque stamp. (This method was first described in chapter 6.) Often one or even several bands of stamped designs are imprinted on a thrown or thrown-and-paddled piece that has been damp tooled (and therefore is in its finished shape). Since stamping requires strong pressure from the inside of a wall, the finger must have access to the area to be stamped. In smaller pieces, this is no problem. In larger, closed pieces, the finished piece should be cut through with an irregular or undulating line, at about shoulder level or to allow sufficient space for the hand to reach in through the new opening. After pressing in the desired designs (the clay must be still malleable or responsive to pressure to permit this), the cut edges are scored and slipped, and the piece put back together.

Later on, in the bisque state, the stamped areas can be stained and wiped, leaving color in the low areas to accentuate surface changes. Stopping out high spots with resist or rubbing glaze off raised areas is another method of doing so.

Glazes

High-fire glazes have direct kinship to igneous rocks as found in nature. The key to their nature is found in feldspathic rock, a common igneous (or "fire-related") rock that melts at the lower margin of stoneware temperatures (2300° F or 1260° C). Thus the simplest high-fire glaze would result from the direct dusting of feldspar on the shoulders of a jar. Equally direct would be the action of a wood fire on a piece of pottery once the temperature moves into the high-fire range, for then the ashes carried by the flame fuse with the clay of the pot, creating a runny glaze.

In the case of both feldspar and wood ash we find the basic ingredients of glazes: silica and some form of flux which acts upon the silica to melt it at a specific temperature. To these the potter often adds clay, which aids in stabilizing the glaze so that it becomes less runny. Feldspar has, in nature, all three of these ingredients: silica, flux, and clay. The varying of their proportions determines the temperature at which a glassy mix results: the larger the amount of silica proportionate to flux, the higher the temperature. Feldspar has six parts of silica to one part of flux, in its usual form. Since this ratio is somewhat high for stoneware glazes, additional flux is usually added to feldspar in studio practice. Other ingredients are added to arrive at effects the potter desires. By itself, a simple feldspathic glaze will result in a surface much like that of the rock itself: whitish to clear to pearly, thick and curdly, highly crackled. This is a virtue, not a defect, in the right place and on the right piece.

Bernard Leach, the late and internationally influential British potter, developed a clear stoneware glaze which is the epitome of simplicity:

one part clay, two parts limestone (calcium carbonate), three parts quartz (silica), four parts feldspar. His equally famous Japanese counterpart, Hamada, developed a more milky clear stoneware glaze which is exactly the same as Leach's except for the omission of the clay. I make use of both of these from time to time. They serve well to introduce the reader to the nature of stoneware glazes.

In classes and on my own I use primarily the whitish ash glaze (semi-opaque, semi-matte), and the Shino glaze (bright, shiny, clear in its basic version) as base glazes. They are uncomplicated, close to nature, ready to respond to knowing application and firing. To these I add a saturated iron glaze (a temmoku) as a liner for some forms, a celadon, and occasionally a copper red and another, more opaque, matte.

Locally obtained limestone, feldspar, clay, and wood ashes could constitute all of one's basic glazes. In an abandoned iron mine near me, I also have access to a full palette of iron-bearing clays for colorants—ochres, umbers, violets, pinks, and reds—and kaolinite. But I am not such a purist that I have qualms about ordering clays, feldspars, and coloring oxides from supply houses. It is simply that local resources can lend much to the spirit and character of the potter's art and reestablish his kinship with potters of far off times and places.

The ingredients used in glazes are typically listed by weight: grams, ounces, pounds. A small batch of glaze would result, for example, from a mix of 10,000 grams of dry ingredients. Once wetted down with water and sieved (to remove lumps), this would yield a glaze in the quantity of a gallon and a quarter, roughly. The consistency is that of a thin cream, so that it coats the finger. (Here I should mention that glazes are always stirred before testing with a finger or before using; otherwise the heavy particles would settle and a clear water film would appear on top).

I usually test each new ash mixture through a number of firings. If it is too runny or dark or shiny, I slowly introduce more kaolin (in equal parts of raw and calcined) to the new batch, until its color and off-white stony, semi-opaque, semi-matte character is achieved. Only then will I begin to blend together an old and new batch of ash glaze. In my working batch are remnants of ash glazes dating back ten years. This continuity with change pleases and supports me.

Typically a potter uses a gram scale for weighing out glazes. These can be set for anything from one gram to 2,000 grams. Finely sieved or ground already when the potter obtains them, the ingredients are weighed out dry. Caution should be taken to avoid breathing dusts when handling or wetting these raw materials. While they are not directly toxic, they contain fine silica, which is injurious to the lungs. Extra caution is used with metallic oxides (such as cobalt oxide) used for colorants. Caution is also advised in handling wood ashes, especially before they are washed, for they contain extremely fine particles of silica as well as lye. (The latter disappears in washing the ashes, a process described later.)

Glazes can be classified according to transparency (clear, semi-clear, opaque), surface (shiny, matte, textured), color, and temperature. Usually transparent glazes are shiny, while opaque glazes can be shiny or matte. A glaze will vary according to the thickness of its application, the kind of clay surface it covers, the kind of firing (electric, gas, oil, wood), the atmosphere of the firing (oxidized—clear, or reduced—smoky), and the kind of kiln it is fired in (size, kind of draft in a flame kiln, and even the placement within the kiln). Some potters will add as well the phases of the moon and planetary movements!

Application

Glazes are applied normally to bisque ware—that is, to pots that are once fired but at a low temperature comparative to their "maturing" temperature. The latter is the temperature at which the clay becomes vitreous or glassy (it will ring when one taps it, and it will no longer absorb water).

Application of glazes is by dipping, pouring, and spraying. Spraying is especially good for larger pieces and also for delicate or finely decorated pieces. Since bisque pots are absorbent, dipping them into a stirred glaze will deposit an even coat fairly quickly. As with anything else in pottery, practice makes for expertise in dipping. I learned in Japan, for example, how to hold a small bowl or cup by the thumb of the right hand on the rim, and the middle finger on the foot, take it completely under the glaze, receive it *already dry,* as it emerges, with the thumb and middle finger of the left hand, set it down and tap the rim with a finger wet with glaze where the right thumb originally rested. Result: a perfectly coated bowl or cup. All it needs in addition is cleaning of the bottom of the foot (so it will not glaze fast to the kiln or kiln shelf).

The inside of a vase or jar is glazed by pouring into it enough glaze to fill it a third or so. Then it is quickly picked up, poured out slowly while rotating the piece until the entire inside is coated. With care and practice, a perfect coating can be achieved without splashing the outside of the piece.

As earlier mentioned, I cover designs with a tightly taped blanket around the form for transportation while green, bisqued (for handling glazing of the inside), and, after spraying on first the glaze and then a protective coat of gum tragacanth solution, before transportation to the high-fire kiln. Otherwise, much of the work of decoration is in danger of smudging.

Below is a list of materials and mixes referred to in this chapter, with additional annotations where needed. The firing range is that appropriate to high-fire stoneware and porcelain. The numbers refer to parts by weight. They can be multiplied or divided for appropriate batch size.

1. Black Slip, Complex

Albany Slip	1500
Cobalt Oxide	75
Manganese Dioxide	125
Flint	50
Ash (Washed)	400
Yellow Ochre	50
Raw (or Burnt) Umber	150
Bally Clay	50
Red Clay	50

Add to the above 1/3 porcelain slip (Kaolin 50, Feldspar 37, Flint 13) to raise temperature (avoids tendency to move under the glaze and softens colors). Usable on damp, dry, bisque, and over the raw glaze.

2. Red Slip

Albany slip	300
Red Iron Oxide	60
Flint	20

With care, usable at all stages, like the black slip above.

3. Black Stain

Albany Slip	260
Cobalt Oxide	24
Red Iron Oxide	24
Manganese Dioxide	25

    Apply thinly. Watch tendency to smear in handling.

4. Blue Slip

Albany Slip	220
Kaolin	150
Cobalt Oxide	7

5. White Slips

	Damp	Dry	Bisque
Kaolin	25	15	5
Ball Clay	25	15	15
Calcined Kaolin	0	20	20
Leadless Frit	0	0	5
Nepheline Syenite	0	0	5
Feldspar	20	20	20
Flint	20	20	20
Zircopax	5	5	5
Borax	5	5	5

    Since borax is water soluble, it should be added to water before the water is added to the other ingredients.

6. Wax Resist

Paraffin	50
Kerosene	50

    Heat paraffin in double boiler, remove from heat when melted, stir in kerosene, return to heat. Heat *only* in double boiler or in a concealed element electric pan or crock for safety. Avoid fumes.

7. Sculptor's Mold Latex Rubber

    Available commercially from:

Platex Mold Rubber
Sculpture House
38 East 30th Street
New York, NY

Wash soap into bristles before using a brush in this. Wash brush frequently with soap and water.

8. Whitish Ash Glaze, Cone 8–10

Ash (washed)	300
Feldspar	350
Kaolin	80
Calcined Kaolin	80
Tin Oxide	30

May run when overfired or applied too thick. Ash glaze is caustic, for it contains lye. To wash ashes, cover them with water, and after stirring, allow ashes to settle and the water to clear under the sludge and foam on top. Decant after skimming off the foam. Repeat the washing cycle several more times. It is never advisable to immerse bare hands in ash glaze for any extended time period. Beyond quick dipping, rubber gloves should be worn as a matter of course. With care, ashes can be weighed, then washed for a batch before remaining materials are blended in, then the whole resieved for final mixing. As mentioned in the text, the proportion of kaolin may have to be adjusted upwards (by addition of equal parts of raw and calcined kaolin) to stabilize color and texture of each batch.

9. Shino Glaze, Cone 9–11

Feldspar	95
Ball Clay	5
Table Salt	3

This is best used over slips. For stiffer versions increase Ball Clay by 5 and decrease Feldspar by 5, up to Feldspar 75, Ball Clay 25, (the stiffest version). Salt remains 3. Iron slips do not work as well with Shino, nor does this glaze *usually* combine well with other glazes. Should not be underfired.

Since this glaze contains salt, it cannot be stored in damp places, or for a long time on bisque pieces before firing. It will also penetrate the body of a piece to some degree, occasionally causing some cracking on forms too thin or subject to too much strain in the firing.

10. Gum Tragacanth Solution

Mix one tablespoon of dry gum powder with about one tablespoon of alcohol (shellac thinner or rubbing alcohol). Make sure all the powder is wetted with the alcohol. Then add a pint of water and shake or stir well. This is for coating powdery glazes prior to decorating or for protecting from smudges in moving pieces around. The solution will keep a week or two before spoiling.

11. Japanese Underglaze Porcelain Blue or *Gosu*

This material, originally obtained from nature in China, is now blended synthetically and commercially in Japan. For a subtler blue, red iron oxide is ground into the *gosu* until a reddish tinted blue-gray raw material occurs. It must be used thinly, like a stain, although its range is greater than stains, more like that of sumi ink painting in terms of value variations.

A note on copper glazes: When being fired, copper-glazed pieces can cause a reddish or purplish blush on other pieces with different glazes in the kiln. At times, this enhances the decoration in an unpredictable way.

All decoration reveals the impact of varied forces: loving and commemorative embellishment; echoes of idiosyncratic and cultural myths and archetypes; responsive dialogue and dance between form, eye, and hand; the encircling of the container by one's personal experience of nature; the extension into and out from the formed surface; the drive toward infinity and immortality opened up when we dwell in the quality of the present; and the humble interpenetration of tradition, life, and the continuous phases of pottery itself. The passage of time is qualitatively and lovingly drawn out by all three levels and accidents of decoration: the firing, the forming, the raised hand with brush and tool.

8

The Kiln

If a potter has clay and a means of firing, he or she is ready for production. A simple pinched pot can be fired, with care, even in an earthen pit with branches and twigs as the fuel. American Indians produced their wares in this fashion. They learned to protect their pieces with bits of broken pottery piled over them, so that the shock of the fire would not be so sudden and intense.

But very early in the history of pottery, kilns were built out of clay bricks and the firing process itself established as a refined art. The Chinese led the way in the production of high-fired wares, both stoneware and porcelain. They were far ahead of Europe in the production of the latter.

There are specialized books on kiln-building, so I will treat the topic in a general way. Since this book concentrates on stoneware and porcelain, I will limit my remarks to high-fire kilns (those firing above cone 8, or around 2300° F or 1260° C).

Kilns can be classified in several different ways: (1) optimal temperature for which they are designed; (2) type of heat (electric, gas, oil, wood); (3) pattern of the heat or flame (up draft, down draft); and firing atmosphere for which they are designed (oxidation, neutral, or reduction). The kilns I have built and used have been high fire (stoneware and porcelain temperatures), have covered the full range of heat sources of fuel, have been both up draft and down draft, and have covered the range of kiln atmospheres. But I have been most at home with gas and oil high-fire kilns, both up draft and down draft, which can easily produce a reduction atmosphere when needed.

Cones—or pyrometric cones—are the potter's visual method of

determining temperature inside the kiln. Cones are stick-like forms, about 3 inches high, made from controlled ceramic ingredients which will bend or tilt as the temperature for which they are designed is reached. The potter sets three of these (or more) in a clay base, usually with a guide cone (lower than the desired temperature), the firing target cone, and a guard cone (to check overfiring). Thus, if I were firing for cone 10, I would set cones 9, 10, and 11 in a row in a cone base. (The higher the number of the cone, the higher the temperature.)

As for heat source, electric heat ordinarily produces only an oxidation, or clear, atmosphere. With gas, oil, or wood, a smoky, or reduction, atmosphere can be obtained in one of two ways (both having the same effect): by cutting down the air or oxygen supply or by introducing more fuel than the available oxygen can easily handle. Without changing fuel ratio, for example, a damper in the flue or chimney, or an air intake in the combustion chamber of the fire box can be partially closed, thus cutting down the amount of available oxygen. Alternatively, all air intakes can be left as they are while more gas, oil, or wood is introduced into the combustion chamber.

An up-draft kiln is self-explanatory: The flame or heat rises from a heat source under the firing chamber, travels through the stacked wares, and exits out of the top of the kiln. The kiln is in effect its own chimney. In a down-draft kiln the flame rises—usually from fire boxes at the bottom and side of the firing chamber where the wares are stacked— and travels to the top of the kiln where, since there is no exit, it descends to the floor of the firing chamber and passes through holes or exits into a flue beneath the chamber, then to a chimney separate from the kiln.

Flames are something like water. They like to be dispersed or spread out or else their force becomes too strong. They prefer to follow rounded surfaces, curving with their natural flow. Thus the top of a kiln is typically an arch, for structural, functional, and aesthetic reasons. Structurally, bricks cannot easily or safely span the open top of a kiln box (the basic kiln shape is often a cube, with some notable exceptions later discussed). The flame flows easily over an arch form, and the structure takes on an architectural beauty all its own.

Up-draft kilns usually have their arched top outside, or beyond, a basic cube form. This makes sense, since the elongation helps carry the flames upward. Down-draft kilns typically have their arch within a cubic form, which caps the flame in, so to speak, forcing it downward.

Kilns are built with ceramic bricks that can withstand temperatures rated *above* the firing temperature desired. These bricks can be either dense or heavy fire-clay type bricks or lightweight, insulation type bricks which have air spaces within them. Often the inner liner and arch of a kiln are made with insulation bricks, for these hold heat (with less radiation effect) and, in the case of the arch, cut down on the weight considerably. Kiln bricks are most commonly regular 9-inch bricks: "straights" for the walls, and "arch" or "wedge" bricks for the arch.

The parts of a kiln, thus, are: fire box, where the heat enters; firing chamber, where the wares are stacked on shelves of suitable high-fire material (such as silica carbide); flue or chimney, where the heat or flame exits. Of course, there must also be a door for loading and unloading and a peephole for checking the course of a firing. I prefer a kiln in which the flame is visible and accessible. If I had my way, kilns would have many blow holes, as they do in Japan, where the flame can be looked into, and where it sticks out its tongue of fire under a reduction atmosphere. Machined kilns with tightly sealed chamber boxes lose the spirit of firing too much for my taste.

I also prefer kilns with a full or Roman arch, full semicircle at the arch back. The almost cathedral-like beauty of the inside of the kiln invites potter and flame to their best effort.

Bisquing can be done in almost any kind of kiln, as long as the atmosphere is kept clear or oxidized. In bisquing larger bowls and other large forms, I was taught in Arita to lift them from the shelf with small coils under the foot rim. Four such coils made from plastic clay, placed at right angles to the foot rim, suffice. This allows heat to circulate around the entire piece. These coils should be thinner than the little finger and still thinner on the inner side of the foot so that they carry as little moisture as possible to the bottom of the piece. It is also advisable not to place anything inside these large forms for bisquing. All of the bisquing is done between 1600° and 1650° F (roughly 870° to 900° C), neither too low for clay strength nor too high for insufficient absorption of glazes.

Once the wares are glazed and collected together, the kiln is ready to load. There are a number of preparatory steps, however, which I will discuss shortly. But first a few more words about kilns. I have built a dozen kilns in my years as a potter, each having a distinct personality and producing its own peculiar effects. The intuitive side of building and firing kilns cannot, from my point of view, be overemphasized. It is not just a matter of technical expertise and ceramic science. Pottery, following the French usage, is one of the "arts of the fire." One must identify with the kiln, the fuel, the flame, and the firing process. At some point, and in depth, the potter must wed his imagination to fire. He must feel its presence even in digging clay, in shaping it, and in decorating it. He must continue to feel that presence as he holds the finished piece in his hands. This can only come from direct engagement of the potter's heart and faith in the firing process.

The work around a kiln can be heavy labor, thus inviting a collaborative effort. Kiln shelves periodically need to be cleaned, chipped of old glaze, and recoated with kiln wash. Bricks for fire walls, holding shelves, and the doorway must be kept in good condition, and replaced when necessary. Fireways and flues must be clear of obstructions. Fallen bits of refractories must be cleaned out, and shelves or spaces for the glazed and ready bisque must allow ease of access and choice of the right shape and size for a tight loading. Stacking the kiln develops an exquisite and precise sense of space. A beginner is surprised to see the number of pieces an experienced potter can place within the firing chamber. As wares are set in place, the mind visualizes the flow of the flame through the kiln and takes into consideration which glazes should be placed high or low, front or back, of the kiln, for temperature and atmosphere will vary according to each kiln, each potter firing, and also according to the stacking pattern.

All of this requires unhurried attention and collaboration. When the kiln is fired, a natural hierarchy of command arises, for, though aided by all, someone must assume the lead, and take responsibility for a total vision of the event. Beginning apprentices at firing a kiln often mistakenly assume that only technical matters need be their concern: how to load, how to light the kiln, when to turn it up, how to regulate the dampers, when to start reduction, and so on. But all of these are just part of a total event called a firing, which goes from loading through firing to unloading and responding to the ware. Care, love, and patience must prevail; selfishness, haste, and outside commitments do not mix with these activities. One must delight in kiln-watching—it is a contemplative and hopeful time—but also must take care not to have a lapse of concentration. It is also a relaxed time. In Japan, kiln watchers often celebrate and drink sake. But it is also a religious time, when the gods are involved.

Unloading should have a joyous but slow rhythm about it, much as participation in a fine dinner. Why a feverish rush to finish? The whole process is one. It should reverberate and telescope from the shovel in the hand at a clay dig, to the finished piece in the hand at the kiln door.

When I fire with students, we take our kiln gods seriously, but in a playful spirit. Once the door is bricked in, the pilots lit, and the door chinks sealed with clay, we undergo another ritual: One of us throws a small pellet of moist clay onto the door bricks, thus establishing a playful mood and releasing the care and attention required to prepare the kiln for firing. Everyone else in the group begins throwing pellets, trying to hit the first pellet, covering it completely. A beautiful scattershot design usually results. And, as in most effort, the student with the most relaxed and centered attitude gains the bull's eye. Such divine folly brings common labor to the mood of celebration.

This is the place to mention a kind of kiln and firing that invites special communal work. The model for this orientation comes from potters' communities in the dim past and reaches us, most recently, through the Orient—in my experience, through Japan, where it is called a *noborigama,* or hill-climbing kiln. The noborigama is exactly what the name implies: a kiln—actually like a series of small connected kilns—which is built on the slope of a hill. Typically such a kiln is a combination up draft and down draft. The entire kiln has an up-draft effect since it ascends a hill; thus the kiln is its own chimney and often has no visible chimney at the top of the hill. But between each chamber or cell in the climbing kiln there is a down-draft effect, for the flame enters through a fire box or stoke hole, climbs to the arched top of the chamber, descends to the uphill bottom side and exits into the next chamber, where the pattern is repeated on to the next chamber. There can be as few as two or three chambers or as many as ten or more.

The bottom chambers reach the target temperature first. Once they do, they are sealed off and the stoking process is moved slowly up the hill until all chambers have reached the appropriate temperature.

In chapter 3, I discussed briefly a communal building of a noborigama undertaken in one of my advanced pottery classes. I was to repeat the hill-climbing kiln experience twice more with advanced classes of pottery students. The last hill-climbing kiln was built on my property, the hill formed by using earth, rubble, stones, cinder blocks, and cement. The kiln had three chambers of about five feet in height, with a special lowered chamber between the second and third regular chambers. This lowered chamber—a *bunkazaibako,* or "cultural treasure box"—came from the Bizen tradition. It is fired differently from the chambers. Instead of stoking into a small door in the chamber itself, as is true with the others (where the fire is moved slowly up the hill as preceding or lower chambers are "fired off" and sealed), at the height of the fire, at its level, pulverized charcoal is sprinkled liberally over the glowing pots. The charcoal adheres at once to the pots, forming large but soft clinkers. After unloading, these clinkers are knocked off, leaving behind a beautifully variegated matte, instead of shiny, ash glaze.

This kiln, which was built under a shed roof, with its upper chamber and chimney out in the open, was the scene for a number of high-fire wood firings. Each of these had its own community quality to it. The buildup of labor and anticipation intensified as wood was collected and sawed and split and stacked. Pots of native clay were brought in and loaded, and the fire slowly started.

Wood firings, in a kiln of this scale, typically go on for several days. The sustained tempo of work and care creates a feeling of participation with fire unknown otherwise. The stoking must be rhythmical, neither too fast (or the kiln will choke with ashes and unburnt wood) nor too slow (or the temperature will fall instead of rise). The wood explodes as soon as it hits the fire box. One piece follows another. Yet there are cycles, for the smoke builds up to a heavy reduction atmosphere, then clears down to neutral, and another cycle begins.

Such firings are humbling and sobering events as well as high points of the spirit. They bring one face to face with the full force of elemental flame. The results that come forth quiet down any excess of zeal we may have for form and decoration. Here the accidents of forming and firing say it all, and set up a scale of nature against which to try our work.

9

Living with Pottery

From earliest times, art and life have been one. Expressive activity, in one form or another, is part of the living creature. In bringing forth something with its own unique quality, we celebrate the qualitative basis of life itself. It is only when our lives are fragmented and desperate that we must talk about art-life connections.

Presence and Place

That which is whole and organic has presence, for when its quality confronts us we dwell fully in the present with it; we find a renewal within our experience. Such an object symbolizes what we are happiest to be: a continuous stream of qualitative wholeness.

When we cannot feel this wholeness in our experience of a pot, then we have chosen not to respond, for whatever reason, or the pot in its very character lacks, for us, the presence of qualitative wholeness. Both man-made and natural places, too, have pervasive character and wholeness. Nature, undisturbed, always seems to have a unity that carries through its every detail, even within the changes of hour and weather and season.

Once, while unloading my outdoor stoneware kiln, in which I had just fired a half-year's continuous work, I began to place the pieces on the ground, amid leaves and grass, on back into the woods. I wanted to see whether the one presence—that of place—could absorb the other presence—of the pots. And could the presence of the pots affect that of place? A synergy, a synchronicity of art and place where we as humans can dwell more fully, is our cultural Garden of Eden. Where the two coexist in mutual enhancement, we have the Tao of art.

The native stoneware clay I have described repeats in its wood-fired or ash-glazed range the presence of the place of its origins. It is like the speckled rhododendron leaf fallen on top of hemlock needles. Its fired, naked clay repeats the subtle colors issuing from the ground itself. Here the piece in its own presence reveals the presence of the place of its origins.

Can we say this of porcelain, too? Man can write on the sun-filled cloud as well as on the earth of the woods. The bright colors on white cotton and silk kimonos have a presence not unlike that of overglazed Arita ware. And the white porcelain stone comes from the ground of Arita.

Place is determined by where we dwell together just as much as where we dwell together is determined by place. One artist who found himself growing in a special environment said that his work there was "like something waiting for a place to happen." His growth made the presence of that place just as much as the place made him grow.

This is the synchronicity and synergy I have alluded to—neither cause nor effect, but a reciprocity beyond these mechanical terms. A good pot creates, even demands or commands, place and space. It is to the indoors what rocks and ferns are to the outdoors.

Beginners must learn the wisdom of delaying judgment, abandoning expectation, and providing a place in which the presence of each pot may happen. Often I tell them to wet their bowl, or take it away, out in the sun; or to take their pots someplace where they feel at ease, and spread them out quietly and lovingly, so that they can begin to adjust to the qualities that are there. The place of presence and the presence of place must collaborate with the human, in very basic, qualitative, phenomenologically experienced art-life connections.

The Sacramental Ritual of Eating and Drinking

I said it clearest in chapter 1: A cup is the sacrament of drink, a bowl the benevolent nurturance of sustenance. We have commerce with cupping and bowling, not with objects at rest.

Attachment to the objects we use daily renders them personally meaningful, but often this is a sentimental attachment. Some cooks know how to create a visual feast in the way food and drinks are prepared and presented, and here again, culture and place and object and occasion fuse into one qualitative event, unrolling in time like a passage of music.

Sensitive Japanese chefs have little regard for sets of cups and dishes. Each piece used is chosen for what it will contain and how it will contribute to a whole composed of many items of food and many dishes. The latter, themselves, are of a surprising variety of form and color, compared with Western standards. There may be a low tray, a small basket, a covered bowl, a small wine cup, a tea cup, a plate, and so on, and each of these will vary according to the style and place of its origin.

Pots are containers. They affect their contents just as their contents affect them, and so they participate in the spiritual and aesthetic dimensions of eating and drinking in such a way that holistic integration of body-mind is encouraged. We are nourished by presence and place, by shared care and love, not just by food. These are all one when the sacramental and ritualistic qualities of eating and drinking are rediscovered (Plates 27–29).

The potter who knows this never just *makes* a cup or a bowl. He or she retains a vision of all that presence can mean when the right piece, place, and occasion unite. No wonder the Japanese expect so much from a ceremonial tea bowl, and no wonder the potter finds these so challenging to make. Yet the humblest and quietest approaches often work best for the highest purposes, for these can partake of the infinite presence of nature itself.

Dissolution of Art-Life Connections: The Gallery, The Museum, and Exhibitions

John Dewey, in *Art as Experience,* points out the detrimental effects on the live creature when art is placed on a pedestal or severed from its connections with life.[1] It is not my intention to convey a negative attitude toward institutions preserving and exhibiting art objects, or educating through them. I myself contribute to museums, have brought back art objects from Japan for a special study collection, and exhibit my own work at galleries, museums, and in varied other exhibitions.

At their best, exhibitions highlight the presence of each art work on display. Skillful control of installation and lighting, in collaboration with the presence of the institution itself, can present us with the object as though in a timeless vacuum, where, as at a concert, it is only the present performance that counts. A magic event unfolds. As with a color transparency by a skilled photographer, we may see only one of an object's many faces, but we see a compelling and highly representative one.

The art of display and presentation is therefore a special and a considerable one, and when we love pots, we adjust ourselves to their presence as institutionalized. That is, we connect a pot back to our lives and to the qualitative life commanded by the presence of the piece itself. Any piece can be isolated in this way: say a small Minoan figure in the center of a large case in a large room in a large museum.

When we forget, however, that art objects have been shorn of their home with certain people in a special time and place, then such displays lead to an overintellectualization and a leveling of quality. Each piece can still "perform," but like an animal in a zoo, its wholeness, and therefore its presence, have been infringed upon. It becomes an endangered species.

This aspect of our modern life, seen phenomenologically, is like watching television. We cannot really participate. We take in more "reality" and "variety" at the expense of genuine experience, where presence and place and the human are all one qualitative event. I know that I, too, have been gripped by a sports event on television, or held in rapt attention by a piece "on display," but it has always been both a pleasure and a shock to walk away from both.

Living with pots without being a "collector" is an art. My wife has the knack of grouping pots here, isolating one there, setting them among green plants, at many levels, but always in a beneficial interaction between piece and place. The dwelling takes us in quietly and peacefully, nourishing us; and we inhabit the dwelling, leaving a trace of our values and our activities. So do pots.

I try to relax around "valuable" pots, using them and sharing them. There is a great profusion of styles and forms and origins in pieces that I use for eating and drinking. No two pieces match, evoking interesting responses from those with whom I share a meal. And a meal is not for only one time and one place: on a table, on the floor, in the living-study area, on the deck, in the studio, on the grass, a meal, so arranged and brought before one, is a gift of love. The varied presences of varied pots makes this quiet and subtle symbolism possible. But use is not just function, even at symbolic heights. A unified pot is always "spiritually functional," and as such humanizes and extends the presence of place. Even broken and cracked pieces can have sufficient presence that they become parts of the landscape. At one time I placed many problem pieces in with a pile of stones in a setting large enough to absorb them into its own natural presence. Moss and leaves further linked the two together.

We live well with pottery, then, when pottery and our lives have no line between them. That the presence of pieces affects our very mood and being can be demonstrated when the pieces are gone, whether at exhibitions, or through a change of hands by sale or gift. When at one point in my life I went through an existential crisis and changed where and how I lived, I thought I could leave everything behind, but reasoned that five loved pieces would be like the seed-bed for a new sense of place, of home, of presence—a kind of continuity across change. We are said to be wealthy by reference to what we can live without, but I would equally say that we are wealthy by reference to the presences and places that shape and nourish us, without reference to value and ownership. The tree outside my studio is legally mine, but its presence belongs to nature.

So I am not a collector but a person who makes and lives with pots. All of life is a gift, and when I make pots or they come to live in my home, that, too, is a gift. Whatever their source historically, we live well with pots when we appreciate them as we appreciate life itself. When the sun strikes them a certain way, or if we view them upon opening our eyes after meditating, we realize that they provide us with improvisations as well as command performances.

Great Pots I Have Known

In keeping with the spirit of the rest of this book, I want to share my reflections on only those pieces that I have come to know intimately.

The values of the kind of discipleship within the Great Tradition that I have been describing should make themselves known in the range of pieces that have crossed my own path. Some of these pieces are "famous" by the art world's standards, others are not. They are still "great," even when anonymous, for what they have taught me.

Many of the pieces described in the following pages have been in my home for years. Even as I write about each piece now, its quality and presence confront me in a way impossible to capture in words. I can only hope to examine some of the textural strands within each qualitative unity, thereby discovering ever new aspects of its wholeness. To do this, I must give the reader some rather pedestrian descriptions as well. But I also hope to come by new interpretations of my own on the way, for my world and the world of each piece is bound together by an understanding that is not static, which telescopes within itself all that this book is trying to say.

Paddled temmoku vase (Plate 30). Bernard Leach, c. 1956. H. 10 in. (25.4 cm.). Collection: The School for American Craftsmen, Rochester Institute of Technology. (Gift of the author.)

This grayish white stoneware vase was paddled into a softly rounded squarish form, swelling outward at its midpoint. The flat, laid-down lip strongly terminates the form, giving it a contained, high-shouldered gesture. Two of its four faces are freely decorated with a strong vertical stroke of a stick, with finer zigzag spiraling lines crossing it, from wide at the top to almost no width at the bottom.

The temmoku glaze is mostly dark, a kind of pinholed eggplant black in color and texture, breaking into iron-red orange over designs, edges of the lip, and raised parts of throwing ridges. One of the faces without a design on it receives a fortuitous pattern from the way the glaze breaks into red orange diagonally over its surface.

This pot is alive and noble, achieving unity through restraint and interaction in form, decoration, glaze, and firing. Unfooted, the base shows the string-cut pattern clearly. The "BL" and "St. Ives" stamps, one on each undecorated side, are visible on the outside bottom.

Molded bottle (Plate 31). Japanese, Kanjiro Kawai, c. 1965. Stoneware. H. 7 in. (17.8 cm.). Collection: Museum of Art, The Pennsylvania State University, from the Japanese Study Collection acquired by the author in 1967 for the University.

Toward the latter part of his artistic career, Kawai experimented with a wide variety of bottles and vases formed by tamping clay slabs into bisque molds. From the side, this piece converges steadily from the base to the outturned lip, and the rounded shoulders construct perfect arches. The entire form, seen straight on, sits strong, secure, almost immovable.

The whole piece has been glazed in a crackly feldspathic ash glaze, grayish white in color. The lip, part of the neck at the top, and a band at the bottom have been dipped in an iron-red temmoku glaze.

Against this stability and solidity, Kawai has flung a musical dance of brush strokes in iron red, underglaze copper red-pink, and *gosu* blue. These play over the form with great animation, almost abandon, the strokes fading out into graded edges, like ribbons against a sunny sky.

Five pieces with impressed rope patterns and brush decorations (Plate 32). Japanese, Tatsuzo Shimaoka, 1967–75. Stoneware. Vase, H. 9 1/8 in (23.2 cm.); plate, D. 10 3/4 in. (27.3 cm.); square bottle, H. 4 1/2 in. (11.3 cm.); triangular bottle, H. 4 1/4 in. (10.7 cm.); cup, H. 3 1/4 in. (8.2 cm.). Collections: vase, Museum of Art, The Pennsylvania State University, a gift of the author and Dr. Joan Novosel-Beittel; remainder, author's collection.

The use of rope impressions in the soft clay is one of Shimaoka's trademarks. He came by it honestly, for his father was a maker of decorative cords—an interesting way of assuring continuity. The rope impressions seen in four of these five pieces vary from piece to piece. The largest patterns occur on the plate, where they spiral into a central circle or "window," on which Shimaoka's somewhat primitive leaf-branch-twig motif appears. This same motif is

30. Paddled temmoku vase. Bernard Leach, c. 1956. H. 10 in. (25.4 cm.).

31. Molded bottle. Japanese, Kanjiro Kawai, c. 1965. Stoneware; H. 7 in. (17.8 cm.).

32. Five pieces with impressed rope patterns and brush decorations. Japanese, Tatsuzo Shimaoka, 1967–75. Stoneware. Vase, H. 9⅛ in. (23.2 cm.); plate, D. 10¾ in. (27.3 cm.); square bottle, H. 4½ in. (11.3 cm.); triangular bottle, H. 4¼ in. (10.7 cm.); cup, H. 3¼ in. (8.2 cm.).

33. Stoneware teapot and salt-glazed jar. American, Robert C. Burkhart, c. 1957, and William Farrell, c. 1966. Teapot, H. (with handle) 7 in. (17.7 cm.); jar, H. 8½ in. (21.6 cm.).

34. Four wood-fired pieces. Three "Penn-yaki," American, anonymous, 1974; Japanese, Rakusai Takahashi, Shigaraki, c. 1967. H. 3½–10 in. (8.9–25.3 cm.).

37. Tightly folded bowl and straight-sided bowl. British, Mary Rogers and John Ward, c. 1975. Rogers, H. 3¾ in. (9.5 cm.); Ward, H. 5⅝ in. (14.3 cm.).

35. Liquor server. Japanese, anonymous, Ryumonji ware, c. 1967. H. (without handle) 2¼ in. (5.7 cm.), D. 6 in. (15.3 cm.).

36. White earthenware incense burner. Japanese, Togei Urushima, c. 1860, white Satsuma ware, Kagoshima. H. (to top of handle) 5½ in. (14 cm.).

38. Four porcelain pieces. American, Nina Gaby (tall cups), and British, Mary White (tall footed bowl), Mary Rogers (delicate pinched bowl), 1977–79. Cups, H. 7½ in. (19 cm.), 6⅜ in. (16.2 cm.); bowls, H. 3⅞ in. (7.3 cm.), 2⅝ in. (6.7 cm.).

39. Nineteen small porcelain bottles, Japanese, anonymous, Arita ware, c. 1800. H. 2¼–3¼ in. (5.8–8.3 cm.).

40. Porcelain bottle. Japanese, anomymous, Ko–
Imari ware, Arita, c. 1800. H. 12¼ in. (31.1 cm.).

41. Small porcelain plate. Japanese Imperial Household ware, Katsuo Tsuji (eleventh generation),
Arita, c. 1861. D. 5⅝ in. (14.9 cm.).

42. Iro-Nabeshima porcelain plate. Japanese, Imaemon
Imaizumi XIII, Arita, c. 1969. D. 8½ in. (21.6 cm.).

43. Porcelain *guinomi* (sake cup). Japanese, Imaemon
Imaizumi XIII, Arita, c. 1980. H. 2½ in. (6.4 cm.).

44. Porcelain ceremonial tea bowl and two sake cups. Japanese, Manji Inoue, Arita, c. 1976. Tea bowl, H. 3¼ in. (8.2 cm.); cups, H. 2 in. (5 cm.).

45. Porcelain incense burner. Japanese, Manji Inoue, Arita, c. 1980. H. 4⅞ in. (12.2 cm.).

46. Large porcelain bowl. Joint work of Manji Inoue
and the author, 1969. D. 21 in. (53.2 cm.).

found on the vase, in a cluster of three, and on the faces of the triangular molded bottle. The rope impressions are all in white, an effect achieved by coating the impressed clay with white slip, then scraping the surface once the slip has set, leaving the white inlaid only in the impressions.

The leaf motif is done with three quick strokes. On the inside of the cup and as the background for the leaf decoration on the triangular molded bottle are quick strokes of *hakeme* white. The glaze is the same on all five pots, a gray, somewhat pearly, semi-transparent feldspathic ash glaze.

These are sturdy, quiet, even comfortable pieces.

Stoneware teapot and salt-glazed jar (Plate 33). American, Robert C. Burkhart, c. 1957, and William Farrell, c. 1966. Teapot, H. (with handle) 7 in. (17.7 cm.); jar, H. 8 1/2 in. (21.6 cm.). Collection: the author.

Here are two strong forms that give some indication of a folk art tradition in America. The teapot is in native Pennsylvania clay, rich, earthern brown, decorated with local iron-bearing slips. Its form is at once daring, sculptural, and elegant. There is a certain mystery and privacy about it, for its openings are small and hidden in proportion to its generous containing capacity. Mostly unglazed on the outside, the pot is accented with three narrow bands of blackish brown slip below its midpoint. The handle is lightly glazed with the same ash glaze discovered on the inside once the concealed lid at the base of the handle is removed.

The shiny surface of the salt-glazed jar comes from a thin vapor glaze. As though to match its companion here, it has a deep black band of slip around its center. The straight sides have loosely spiralling grooves, and one side is wetly brushed with a runny white slip that fades imperceptibly into the warm brown salt-glaze tones. The top lip and matching pinched collar on the shoulder flare out generously, singing of the spontaneity of the spinning wheel and the relaxed hand.

Both pieces speak of earth and daily use without extra refinements.

Liquor server (Plate 34). Japanese, anonymous, Ryumonji ware, c. 1967. H. (without handle) 2 1/4 in. (5.7 cm.), D. 6 in. (15.3 cm.). Collection: Museum of Art, The Pennsylvania State University, from the Japanese Study Collection acquired by the author in 1967 for the university.

This teapot-like server for the strong local distilled spirits is glazed with a textured blackish iron glaze over the red-brown clay body. The flattened body is raised on three pointed feet. It has a rustic, complementing dark-brown reed handle. The bottle form gains visual distinction through its severity and squatness. Pieces like this were distinctly anonymous, everyday, folk art, very inexpensive at the time they were acquired.

Four wood-fired pieces (Plate 35). Three "Penn-yaki," American, anonymous, 1974; Japanese, Takahashi Rakusai, Shigaraki, c. 1967. H. 3 1/2 –10 in. (8.9–25.3 cm.). Collection: the author.

The two smallest pieces are from a summer communal venture when my advanced pottery class dug native clay, made pots, and fired them in a wood-fired *noborigama* consisting of four chambers. These pieces were from a smaller "pinched" chamber between the top two chambers (the *bunkazai-bako,* or cultural treasure box, discussed at length in chapter 8). This caused a clinker-like surface, discernible on both pieces. If one desires, these "barnacles" can be knocked off to reveal a matte surface glaze underneath, but here, they have been left in place to record the transformational power of the entire process.

The third Penn-yaki piece is from a sawdust firing, at a much lower temperature, which produces a fragile clay body, barely beyond bisque, with fire markings much like those on pit- and bonfire-fired American Indian pots. This is an informal but ritualistic goblet-like cup—it has a natural directness and noble restraint about it.

Rakusai's flask-like bottle was obviously flattened while the clay was quite wet, for the surfaces undulate from pressure into the soft sides. Two "ears" are casually pinched out of its shoulders. The entire form is subtly asymmetrical. The foot has been hollowed into a foot ring on the bottom by quick parings with a bamboo knife.

Sizable chunks of flint and feldspar pit and break out from the bottle's surface. These are called *ishihaze,* or stone eruptions, caused by the angular flint and the softened, partially melted rounded half-pearls of the feldspar. The flame-flashed side is a light warm grayish white, textured with reddish browns and blackened toward the foot.

The surfaces of all four pieces are on the first and second levels of decoration: forming and firing. Though the potter cooperates, the "intentional decoration" here belongs to the flame.

White earthenware incense burner (Plate 36). Japanese, Togei Urashima, c. 1860, White Satsuma ware, Kagoshima. H. (to top of handle) 5 1/2 in. (14 cm.). Collection: the author.

Extraordinarily fragile, this incense burner in the shape of a cricket cage has something of the feeling of delicately carved ivory. It is a warm, buff white (aptly called an ivory white) as opposed to the cool white whites of Japanese porcelains of this era. It is covered with a finely crackled transparent glaze. Its feeling of fragility is enhanced by its light weight and the non-vitreous character of the clay.

The form is exquisite, with its handle, a tall oval, expanding at the base to form a wide nest for the body proper, which is a spherical ovoid nestling in its protective embrace. Four points grow out from the curved bottom to become tiny feet, raising the airy shape from the ground. Materials other than clay probably created the details on handle and knob.

This is an example of virtuosity on the part of its maker; a piece of great delicacy, spatial and formal clarity, and poetic charm.

Tightly folded bowl and straight-sided bowl (Plate 37). British, Mary Rogers and John Ward, c. 1975. Rogers, H. 3 3/4 in. (9.5 cm.); Ward, H. 5 5/8 in. (14.3 cm.). Collection: the author.

These two pieces, when viewed together, admirably highlight qualities unique to each. In the case of Mary Rogers' tightly folded bowl, the warmth of the ivory white is increased by the fragile, almost parchment-like translucency of the thin porcelain. This translucent warmth is contrasted by an opaque, grayer color where the thin overlapping folds of the porcelain reveal the increased structural thickness of the piece. These overlaps never seem to repeat, but collect themselves into a perfectly formed hemispherical bowl, from the outside, as though the perfection of a flower could be carved into exquisitely thin marble. The uneven rim is a perfectly organic and natural revelation of its construction—all of a piece and returned to something more like the flower world than that of pots. In short, it is poetic, feminine, an airy hybrid between nature and culture.

John Ward's straight-sided bowl, with its white matte glaze over a partially exposed body, pulls us back into the opacity and "groundedness" of stoneware. This is true even though the piece is highly controlled in form and thinly potted. The glaze and clay are so compatible that one must look at the concealed foot to learn that the clay is a grayish tan color. Then one sees that the clay subtly bleeds through the off-white matte glaze, giving it specks and striations of tan. The effect is remarkably sculptural, even architectural. Both pieces are a visual and tactile feast.

Four porcelain pieces (Plate 38). American, Nina Gaby (tall cups), and British,

Mary White (tall footed bowl) and Mary Rogers (delicate pinched bowl), 1977–79. Cups, H. 7 1/2 in. (19 cm.), 6 3/8 in. (16.2 cm.); bowls, H. 3 7/8 in. (7.3 cm.), 2 5/8 in. (6.7 cm.). Collection: the author.

Here are four porcelains which are quite removed from the Arita tradition. Mary White's tall footed bowl perhaps has an echo of ancient China in it, but the other pieces seem to break free from the East. Mary Rogers's delicate pinched bowl is as fragile as a flower in the hand, and it asks to be held that way—lightly and tenderly in the fingertips. Its tawny semi-matte glaze breaks into rose- and peach-colored speckles irregularly. As though to define its outer limits, the paper-thin deckled edge is colored a brownish black at the very rim. The whole piece is so light and has such a small foot that a passing breeze literally, as well as visually, shakes it. The tender care and the life of the pinching fingers can be felt in the fragile wall. It is airy, feminine, almost ethereal.

In contrast, the thinly potted tall footed bowl by Mary White seems sturdy, but it is really quite light. The pale-blue semi-matte interior glaze breaks into a flecked tan on much of the exterior. Its tall foot has been built up with flattened coils which add a nice decorative detail in the way they loop and circle together, for the coils have been left unfused and stained within their grooves to further accentuate the designs they form. The two bowls complement each other beautifully in color and visual weight. The tall footed bowl has an enduring quality, while the delicate pinched bowl seems almost ephemeral—again, like a blossom at its fullest.

The two tall cups are thicker than Mary Rogers's piece, but they too show a delicate touch in hand building. The actual cup hollow is only as deep as the bulge where the base of the handles join, so that these are actually like goblets in that their containing capacity is lifted up, suggesting refinement, special occasion, and ceremony. They are made for rare drink. Cups and bases are carefully constructed from thin porcelain slabs, overlapping at the very line where the handles fall. The smaller cup is glazed from handle down in celadon, with delicate horizontal grooves and circles showing where the glaze pools. The milky white upper part retains a celadon-like texture and luminosity. The taller piece is completely in this latter glaze, which pools into cooler tones, except for the interior of the actual cup, which is a soft purplish pink to raspberries-and-cream purple. Delicate grooves and heart shapes appear under the glaze on the lower part, considerably softened by the luminous, bubbly quality of the milky glaze, which inclines toward pale celadon blue as it thickens. Two hearts in relief accent the upper join of the flowing handle, which takes an added playful loop at the lower join.

Together, these four pieces sing of the delicacy, femininity, and subtle soft color palette that porcelain permits.

Nineteen small porcelain bottles (Plate 39). Japanese, anonymous, Arita ware, c. 1800. H. 2 1/4–3 1/4 in. (5.8–8.3 cm.). Collection: the author.

In 1967, I bought a number of "kiln faults" like these for only a few cents each from an old woman who brought them in a basket each morning to the large pottery festival held in Arita each May. They fascinate me and give me a feeling of kinship with the anonymous early Arita potters who made them. Like them, I have had my problems with firings; and yet, even the "faults" have character and staying power.

Far from the brilliant milk white of contemporary Arita pieces, the color of these old pieces ranges from warm off-whites through grayish whites to bluish, celadon-like whites. The decorations are still in use, but they vary, like calligraphy, with each act of making, and are further accommodated by form and fire.

Throwing lines are visible on the exposed interiors, which are often left unglazed. The "faults" show that here a piece stuck to another, there a piece fell over into kiln rubble (or onto small flint rocks in use before aluminum oxide was used as "placing" material to prevent pieces from sticking to the shelves), and still another may have been damaged in unloading.

Porcelain bottle (Plate 40). Japanese, anonymous, Ko–Imari ware, Arita, c. 1800. H. 12 1/4 in. (31.1 cm.). Collection: Museum of Art, The Pennsylvania State University, from the Japanese Study Collection acquired by the author in 1967 for the university.

This strong bottle shape is decorated in *gosu* or underglaze blue in the *tako karakusa,* or octopus scroll, pattern. The design follows general principles in its major subdivisions, but shows great freedom and sensitivity in the way the spirals, and spirals from spirals, accommodate each other and the overall form. The visual result is one of restful complexity and unity. The glaze has a bluish iridescent cast where it thickens, and the porcelain color is in general much less white than contemporary Arita ware.

Small porcelain (Plate 41). Japanese Imperial Household ware, Katsuo Tsuji (eleventh generation), Arita, c. 1861. D. 5 5/8 in. (14.9 cm.). Collection: the author.

Actually a sample of wares made for the Imperial Palace, this plate is quite thinly thrown and tooled, and decorated with stylized sixteen-petal chrysanthemums, the emperor's exclusive seal. The brushwork shows consummate skill, for the curves and straight lines are without flaw, with no variation in color—not easy to achieve when painting with *gosu* on underglaze bisque, for the brush cannot be tiny or strokes will vary in color. Thus a larger brush is used, and the touch of the pointed tip must be sure and constantly moving. The color of the blue is a paler, grayed blue, as often found in earlier Arita ware. The counter-curling scrolls with sprouting leaves are repeated on the outside of the small plate.

Iro-Nabeshima porcelain plate (Plate 42). Japanese, Imaemon Imaizumi XIII, Arita, c. 1969. D. 8 1/2 in. (21.6 cm.). Collection: the author.

Here is an example of continuity comparable to that of the Kakiemon studio, for the Nabeshima line also runs back thirteen generations. Nabeshima designs are typically more crowded than those of Kakiemon, but are no less poetic. Also, the Nabeshima glazes have a darker and cooler cast.

This plate illustrates the subtle way in which underglaze *gosu* blue can be integrated with overglaze enamels. Except for buds and flowers, all of the elements are outlined first, on the bisque, with the underglaze *gosu* blue. In addition, many larger and smaller leaves and stalks are filled in with varying shades of gosu blue that are lighter than the outlines; then translucent overglaze colors fill in still other leaves and stalks, letting gosu lines shine through them. Finally, the flowers and buds are brushed in with opaque red overglaze, shaded off here and there with red outlines and detail. The colors and forms on this plate seem actually to float on different levels, with different weights— a lushness not unlike the tropics is the result.

Porcelain guinomi (sake cup) (Plate 43). Japanese, Imaemon Imaizumi XIII, Arita, c. 1980. H. 2 1/2 in. (6.4 cm.). Collection: the author.

The Japanese culture is rich in set forms, each of which, like those in poetry, invites ever new versions and insures a ready audience. In scale, the *guinomi* form is akin to large sake cup.

Similar to a large sake cup, this simple, footed, straight-sided cylindrical cup has been lovingly embellished. Right under the lip and above the foot, two lines of underglaze blue set off a decorative panel, with a ground of extremely delicate, painted vertical lines—so close together that 18 lines fall within one inch (2.5 cm.). Set upon this ground is a garland of red poppies with liquid blue-green leaves. The outlines and veins of the leaves, and the centers of the flowers, are also in underglaze blue.

The red of the flowers and the translucent blue-green of the leaves are overglaze enamels. While the leaves are shiny, the flowers are matte with borders of white (from the base porcelain glaze), so that they seem to float forward as they spiral from bottom to top—no less than thirteen flowers appearing in this upward flowing garland.

In this small piece, the color orchestration and subtle spatiality of layers and textures of decorative elements for which Imaemon is world-famous come into harmonious display. This piece is especially meaningful to me, for I acquired it on a visit to Imaemon's studio soon after he had purchased a small bowl of mine from my exhibition then at the Bunkakan in Arita.

Porcelain ceremonial tea bowl and two sake cups (Plate 44). Japanese, Manji Inoue, Arita, c. 1976. Tea bowl, H. 3 1/4 in. (8.2 cm.), cups, H. 2 in. (5 cm.). Collection: the author.

Completely white—a glowing cool white—this ceremonial tea bowl is at first a shock, for my associations run to the anonymous, the natural and the quiet nature of most of the ceremonial tea bowls I have known. But just as snow reflects all colors and changing lights, so does this piece. It teases my imagination to envision what other utensils and mood objects might go with it in an actual tea ceremony. Perhaps everything else might have to be near white, or a daring black, to harmonize or complement this bowl as a focus. There is something very different about the best modern Arita porcelain—its high whiteness is unmatched anywhere else in the world.

In the hands, however, the piece shows its continuity with other tea ceremony bowls. The sides, at first thought to be so straight, ripple sensuously under the fingers, for only fingertips have touched the walls—there was no rib, no tooling. The varying thickness of the walls causes a subtle gradation of whites, while the shadows of one's fingers are discernible through the partially translucent porcelain. On the one side, direct, knowing strokes from the carving-decorating *kanna* have formed a bamboo branch and a cluster of leaves. The leaves stand out sculpturally, formed by a cut which is sharp on the inside (defining the edge of the leaf) and softly beveled away toward the background. Yet all of this subtle detail, including the veining of the leaves with a stroke from a rounded wooden comb, is all but indiscernbile until the light catches it, almost like a watermark on fine paper.

The foot is in typical Manji Inoue style: sturdy, definite, robust. It is almost a logical contradiction, yet it integrates beautifully.

In these delicate sake cups the liquid light of modern Arita porcelain is shown at its best. On one side a bamboo stem, branch and leaf cluster—created with twelve sure strokes of the decorating *kanna*—sets forth a veritable light show. The forms glow, and the interiors of stems and leaves appear darker than they are.

Here the feet flow right into the body of the cups, catching a subtle gradation of glowing light and shadow. In holding these and studying them, I begin to understand why Sensei works almost completely in the white-white porcelain and the white-white ash glaze. A universe of subtleties is at hand.

Porcelain incense burner (Plate 45). Japanese, Manji Inoue, Arita, c. 1980. H. 4 7/8 in. (12.2 cm.). Collection: the author.

This is a modern version of a traditional Japanese form. A deep foot is left, first tooled into a foot rim then carefully cut through in such a way that three rounded feet remain. The innermost part of the bottom of the piece is slightly recessed. This is signed in underglaze blue (*gosu*). The entire surface of the three feet is glazed, including the tip, for the piece is fired on a raised stand or *hama*.

The piece has a precisely fitting lid, set into an unglazed recess at the top of the body. It is crowned with a bud-like knob made from a press mold and attached, when lid and knob are completely dry, by wetting and working up a local slip right at the join. Three cloud-like forms, composed of three overlapping circles—the same form as the feet but here pointing upward—perforate the lid to allow the incense to burn.

Having made versions of these, I know that they require a great deal of detailed work. In this piece, no decoration, no carving, intrudes upon the pristine purity of the unembellished white for which my teacher is widely known. It takes on surrounding lights and forms in the environment, but asks for its own space to reveal its modulated whites and hint at its subtly illuminated interior.

Large porcelain bowl (Plate 46). Joint work of Manji Inoue and the author, 1969. D. 21 in. (53.2 cm.). Collection: the author and Manji Inoue.

My teacher made this bowl during a public demonstration at The Pennsylvania State University in the spring of 1969; it became collaborative when he asked me to tool, decorate, and fire it. I coated the inside with underglaze *gosu* blue on the green ware, and made the design by sgraffito, but with a careful, shallow cut. The design is big and bold—it has trees, plants, waves, flowers, and clouds cutting through a series of narrow circular bands. A light pattern falls over the design, like a cloud passing over a landscape, so that if a form is light outside the demarcation line, it becomes dark within it, and vice versa.

I conclude the book with this piece as a symbol of East-West interaction in an art that knows no time or place, yet reflects each time, place, and maker. This piece also marks a turning point between influence and independence, for as potters we exist in the clearing between these extremes—in the company of the Great Tradition.

When I teach beginners, there is much I cannot show them in their first and second years. In the third year, there is much for which they are preparing. In the fourth year, good students can sense something of what I cannot say, and in the fifth, inner vision begins to awaken. A tension develops between thought and action in the sixth year, and during the seventh year, despair sets in at the passage of time. In the eighth year, students are lost in clay, and by the ninth year, they are ready to take up their apprenticeship within the Great Tradition.

Notes

Preface

1. Bly, Robert. *News of the Universe.* San Francisco: Sierra Club Books, 1980 (Poem of Kabir, version by Robert Bly, p. 272)
2. Vithoulkas, George. *Homeopathy: Medicine of the New Man.* New York: Arco Publishing Co., 1981, p. 110.
3. Wilber, Ken. *Up from Eden.* Garden City, New York: Anchor Press/ Doubleday, 1981.

Introduction

1. Wilhelm, R. *The I Ching.* London: Routledge & Kegan Paul, 1968.
2. Coper, Hans. *Collingwood, Coper.* London: Victoria and Albert Museum, 1969 (catalogue).
3. Stevens, Wallace. *The Collected Poems of Wallace Stevens.* New York: Alfred A. Knopf, 1954, p. 76.
4. Leach, Bernard. *A Potter's Portfolio.* New York: Pitman Publishing Corporation, 1951, p. 16.

Chapter 2

1. Hisamatsu, Shin'ichi. *Zen and the Fine Arts.* Tokyo: Kodansha International, 1971, p. 7.
2. *Ibid.,* pp. 52–60.
3. Suzuki, Daisetz T. *Zen and Japanese Culture.* New York: Bollingen, Princeton University Press, 1959, p. 16

129

4. *Ibid.*, p. 435; from "The Swordsman and the Cat," taken from an old book on swordplay.

5. *Ibid.*, p. 286.

6. Heidegger, Martin. *Poetry, Language, Thought.* New York: Harper and Row, 1971.

7. Sōgen, Ōmori and Katsujō, Terayama. *Zen and the Art of Calligraphy,* trans. John Stevens. London: Routledge & Kegan Paul, 1983.

8. *Ibid.*, p. 4.

9. Herrigel, Eugen. *Zen in the Art of Archery.* New York: Pantheon Books, 1953.

10. *Ibid.*, p. vii.

11. Ponge, Françis. *The Voice of Things,* trans. Beth Archer. New York: McGraw Hill, 1979.

CHAPTER 3

1. Buber, Martin. *I and Thou.* Edinburgh: T. and T. Clark, 1937.

2. Arendt, Hannah. *The Human Condition.* New York: Doubleday and Company (Anchor Books), 1959.

3. Heidegger, Martin. *Poetry, Language, Thought.* New York: Harper and Row, 1971.

CHAPTER 4

1. Dychtwald, Ken. *Bodymind.* New York: Pantheon Books, 1977.

2. Feldenkrais, Moshe. *Awareness Through Movement.* New York: Harper and Row, 1972.

3. Herrigel, Eugen. *Zen in the Art of Archery.* New York: Vintage Books, 1971.

4. Murphy, Michael. *Golf in the Kingdom.* New York: Delta Books, 1972.

5. Gallwey, W. Timothy. *The Inner Game of Tennis.* New York: Random House, 1974.

6. Polanyi, Michael. *The Tacit Dimension.* New York: Anchor Books, 1967.

CHAPTER 7

1. Gadamer, Hans-Georg. *Truth and Method.* New York: The Seabury Press, 1975, p. 36.

2. *Ibid.*, pp. 109–110.

CHAPTER 9

1. Dewey, John. *Art as Experience.* New York: Capricorn Books, 1958.

Bibliography

Bertherat, Therese and Bernstein, Carol. *The Body Has Its Reasons*. New York: Pantheon Books, 1977.

Buber, Martin. *Between Man and Man*. London: Routledge and Kegan Paul, 1947.

Day Elmer S. A Study of Dreams and Dreaming and the Transformation of Dream Themes into Drawings and Paintings. Unpublished Ph. D. Thesis, 1976. University Park, Pa.: The Pennsylvania State University.

Duberman, Martin. *Black Mountain, An Exploration in Community*. New York: E.P. Dutton, 1972.

Heidegger, Martin. *Discourse on Thinking*. New York: Harper and Row, 1966.

Joy, W. Brugh. *Joy's Way*. Los Angeles: J.P. Tarcher, Inc., 1978.

Peckham, Morse. *Man's Rage for Chaos*. Philadelphia: Chilton Book Company, 1965.

Pelletier, Kenneth R. *Mind as Healer, Mind as Slayer*. New York: Delta Books, 1977.

Paper, Stephen C. *World Hypotheses*. Berkeley: University of California Press, 1970.

Ricoeur, Paul. *The Philosophy of Paul Ricoeur*. Boston: Beacon Press, 1978.

Roszak, Theodore. *Unfinished Animal*. New York: Harper and Row, 1975.

Satchidananda, Swami. *Beyond Words*. New York: Holt, Rinehart and Winston, 1977.

Watts, Alan. *In My Own Way*. New York: Vintage Books, 1973.

———. *The Two Hands of God*. New York: Collier Books, 1969.

The "weathermark" identifies this book as a production of Weatherhill, Inc., publishers of fine books on Asia and the Pacific. Book design and typography: Miriam F. Yamaguchi. Layout of photographs: Yutaka Shimoji. Production supervision: Mitsuo Okado. Composition, printing, and binding: Korea Textbook, Seoul. The typeface used is Monotype Bembo.